© **Copyright 2021 - All rights reserved.**

The content contained within this book may not be reproduced, duplicated or transmitted without direct written permission from the author or the publisher.

Under no circumstances will any blame or legal responsibility be held against the publisher, or author, for any damages, reparation, or monetary loss due to the information contained within this book, either directly or indirectly.

Legal Notice:

This book is copyright protected. It is only for personal use. You cannot amend, distribute, sell, use, quote or paraphrase any part, or the content within this book, without the consent of the author or publisher.

Disclaimer Notice:

Please note the information contained within this document is for educational and entertainment purposes only. All effort has been executed to present accurate, up to date, reliable, complete information. No warranties of any kind are declared or implied. Readers acknowledge that the author is not engaged in the rendering of legal, financial, medical or professional advice. The content within this book has been derived from various sources. Please consult a licensed professional before attempting any techniques outlined in this book.

By reading this document, the reader agrees that under no circumstances is the author responsible for any losses, direct or indirect, that are incurred as a result of the use of the information contained within this document, including, but not limited to, errors, omissions, or inaccuracies.

Table of Contents

Introduction 14

Chapter 1: The Plant-Based Smoothie and Juice Magic 16
    Benefits of A Smoothie and Juicing Lifestyle 17
    Juicing Vs. Smoothies 22
    Blending and Juicing Rules to Follow 23
    How to get the most benefits out of juicing or blending 24
    Going Dairy Free 25

Chapter 2: Ingredients to a Healthier You 26
    Top 8 Greens for Your Smoothies 27
    Best Vegetables for Your Smoothies 28
    Best Medical Herbs You Can Add to Smoothies 29
    Top Fruits for Your Smoothies 30
    Top Vegetables for Juicing 38
    Top Fruits for Juicing 38
    Herbs, Spices, Mix-Ins 39
    How to Wash Your Produce 39
    How to Prepare Your Produce 40
    What to Do with The Pulp After Juicing 42

Chapter 3: The Essential Kitchen Tools for Smoothies and Juices 43
    Selecting the Best Blender 44
    Soaking Your Nuts, Oats, And Seeds 46
    How to Store Your Smoothies 47
    Juicing Tools 48
    Selecting the Best Juicer 49
    How to Store Your Juices 51

Chapter 4: Plant-Based Smoothie & Juicing Recipes 52
Breakfast Smoothies 53
    Almond Smoothie 54
    Banana Oatmeal Smoothie 54

Apple Oatmeal Smoothie	55
Strawberry Oatmeal Smoothie	55
Blackberry & Spinach Smoothie	56
Mixed Berries Smoothie	56
Pineapple & Mango Smoothie	57
Kiwi & Banana Smoothie	57
Orange Smoothie	58
Green Hemp Smoothie	58

Brain Nourishing Smoothies 59

Mocha Chia Smoothie	60
Chocolate Banana Smoothie	60
Blueberry & Avocado Smoothie	61
Berries, Kale & Avocado Smoothie	61
Limony Blackberry Smoothie	62
Turmeric Fruity Smoothie	62
Kale & Avocado Smoothie	63
Nutty Spinach Smoothie	63
Broccoli, Kale & Apple Smoothie	64
Green Pumpkin Seed Smoothie	64

Smoothies to Protect Your Bones & Kidneys 65

Blueberry Smoothie	66
Blueberry & Cucumber Smoothie	66
Strawberry & Bell Pepper Smoothie	67
Cranberry Smoothie	67
Raspberry & Peach Smoothie	68
Pineapple Smoothie	68
Cherry & Blueberry Smoothie	69
Peach Smoothie	69
Kale & Pineapple Smoothie	70
Cabbage & Cucumber Smoothie	70

Anti-Aging Smoothies 71
    Chocolate Date Smoothie 72
    Banana & Blackberries Smoothie 72
    Pear & Cherry Smoothie 73
    Strawberry & Pistachio Smoothie 73
    Raspberry & Kale Smoothie 74
    Raspberry & Blackberry Smoothie 74
    Blackberry & Strawberry Smoothie 75
    Watermelon & Apple Smoothie 75
    Papaya Smoothie 76
    Lettuce & Banana Smoothie 76

Antioxidant Smoothies 77
    Spirulina Blueberry Smoothie 78
    Berries & Beet Smoothie 78
    Fruity Beet Smoothie 79
    Raspberry & Pomegranate Smoothie 79
    Pomegranate, Cherries & Cabbage Smoothie 80
    Blueberry & Pomegranate Smoothie 80
    Chocolate Raspberry Smoothie 81
    Strawberry, Celery & Greens Smoothie 81
    Kale & Cucumber Smoothie 82
    Kale & Celery Smoothie 82

Cleansing Smoothies 83
    Spiced Smoothie 84
    Pineapple & Turmeric Smoothie 84
    Pineapple & Cucumber Smoothie 85
    Cranberry & Grapefruit Smoothie 85
    Watermelon & Strawberry Smoothie 86
    Pineapple & Grapefruit Smoothie 86
    Berries & Pomegranate Smoothie 87
    Herbed Greens Smoothie 87
    Minty Green Smoothie 88
    Spinach & Banana Smoothie 88

Diabetic Smoothies ... 89
- Strawberry & Spinach Smoothie ... 90
- Avocado & Mint Smoothie ... 90
- Spinach & Avocado Smoothie ... 91
- Matcha Chia Seed Smoothie ... 91
- Greens & Cucumber Smoothie ... 92
- Zucchini & Spinach Smoothie ... 92
- Cucumber & Parsley Smoothie ... 93
- Green Sunflower Butter Smoothie ... 93
- Baby Greens Smoothie ... 94
- Green Veggies Smoothie ... 94

Digestive Improvement Smoothies ... 95
- Blueberry & Beet Smoothie ... 96
- Blueberry & Pineapple Smoothie ... 96
- Pineapple Smoothie ... 97
- Pear Smoothie ... 97
- Peach Smoothie ... 98
- Peach, Pear & Papaya Smoothie ... 98
- Papaya Smoothie ... 99
- Papaya & Carrot Smoothie ... 99
- Carrot & Orange Smoothie ... 100
- Green Date Smoothie ... 100

High-Energy Smoothies ... 101
- Date & Almond Smoothie ... 102
- Nutty Banana Smoothie ... 102
- Banana Peanut Butter Smoothie ... 103
- Raspberry Peanut Butter Smoothie ... 103
- Berries Smoothie ... 104
- Kiwi & Melon Smoothie ... 104
- Sweet Potato & Orange Smoothie ... 105
- Pumpkin & Banana Smoothie ... 105
- Matcha, Spinach & Pineapple Smoothie ... 106
- Greens & Carrot Smoothie ... 106

Green Smoothies ... 107

- Mint Smoothie ... 108
- Avocado Smoothie ... 108
- Grapes & Swiss Chard Smoothie ... 109
- Pear & Spinach Smoothie ... 109
- Apple & Avocado Smoothie ... 110
- Lemon Kale Smoothie ... 110
- Kiwi, Grapes & Kale Smoothie ... 111
- Green Fruity Smoothie ... 111
- Cucumber & Lettuce Smoothie ... 112
- Lettuce & Avocado Smoothie ... 112

Healthy Skin Smoothies ... 113

- Peach & Aloe Vera Smoothie ... 114
- Orange, Kiwi & Carrot Smoothie ... 114
- Sweet Potato & Mango Smoothie ... 115
- Sweet Potato & Carrot Smoothie ... 115
- Raspberry Date Smoothie ... 116
- Mango & Cashew Smoothie ... 116
- Mixed Fruit Smoothie ... 117
- Tomato Smoothie ... 117
- Fruity Spinach & Lettuce Smoothie ... 118
- Kale, Avocado & Fruit Smoothie ... 118

Kid-Friendly Smoothies ... 119

- Banana Smoothie ... 120
- Pistachio Banana Smoothie ... 120
- Mango & Walnut Smoothie ... 121
- Strawberry Date Smoothie ... 121
- Mocha Smoothie ... 122
- Chocolaty Oats Smoothie ... 122
- Chocolaty Seeds Smoothie ... 123
- Chocolaty Strawberry Smoothie ... 123
- Chocolaty Cherry Smoothie ... 124
- Apple & Spinach Smoothie ... 124

Low-Fat Smoothies 125
Strawberry & Plum Smoothie 126
Greens & Orange Smoothie 126
Kiwi & Cucumber Smoothie 127
Raspberry, Cabbage & Tomato Smoothie 127
Melon & Cucumber Smoothie 128
Guava & Pineapple Smoothie 128
Apricot & Raspberry Smoothie 129
Watermelon & Cucumber Smoothie 129
Coconut Green Smoothie 130
Cranberry, Pear & Orange Smoothie 130

Protein-Packed Smoothies 131
Peanut Butter Smoothie 132
Vanilla Smoothie 132
Apple Smoothie 133
Raspberry Smoothie 133
Mango Tofu Smoothie 134
Strawberry Smoothie 134
Maca Smoothie 135
Kiwi Smoothie 135
Fruity Tofu Smoothie 136
Pumpkin Smoothie 136
PB&J Smoothie 137
Healthy Protein Coffee Smoothie 137

Weight-Loss Smoothies 138
Cherry Smoothie 139
Carrot, Tomato & Celery Smoothie 139
Peach & Mango Smoothie 140
Strawberry & Orange Smoothie 140
Melon Smoothie 141
Melon & Mango Smoothie 141
Pear, Grapes & Kale Smoothie 142
Apple, Pear & Avocado Smoothie 142

Spinach, Strawberry & Orange Smoothie	143
Apple, Cucumber & Spinach Smoothie	143

Chapter 5: Plant-Based Juicing Recipes ... 144

Brain Healthy Juices ... 145

Blueberry Juice	146
Strawberry & Apple Juice	146
Berries & Carrot Juice	147
Cranberry, Apple & Orange Juice	147
Carrot Juice	148
Carrot, Beet & Spinach Juice	148
Matcha Green Juice	149
Kale, Carrot & Grapefruit Juice	149
Apple, Kale & Cucumber Juice	150
Citrus & Ginger Green Juice	150

Cleansing & Detoxifying Juices ... 151

Orange Juice	152
Orange & Carrot Juice	152
Grapefruit, Apple & Carrot Juice	153
Apple Juice	153
Apple & Carrot Juice	154
Apple & Pomegranate Juice	154
Apple, Orange & Broccoli Juice	155
Red Fruit & Veggies Juice	155
Celery, Carrot & Orange Juice	156
Cucumber, Apple & Carrot Juice	156

Digestive Health Juices ... 157

Watermelon Juice	158
Pomegranate Juice	158
Pineapple, Orange & Carrot Juice	159
Pineapple & Spinach Juice	159
Cucumber & Celery Juice	160

Heart Healthy Juices 161
Strawberry & Walnut Juice 162
Berries & Apple Juice 162
Green Fruit Juice 163
Apple, Celery & Ginger Juice 163
Kale & Orange Juice 164

Immunity Boost Juices 165
Blueberry, Beet & Apple Juice 166
Apple, Beet & Carrot Juice 166
Citrus Spinach & Celery Juice 167
Beet & Carrot Juice 167
Kale, Carrot & Apple Juice 168

Internal/ Structure Supporting Juices 169
Swiss Chard, Apple & Orange Juice 170
Red Fruit Juice 170
Kale, Celery & Pear Juice 171
Mixed Veggies Juice 171
Spinach, Celery, Apple & Orange Juice 172

Green Juices 173
Apple, Cucumber & Kale Juice 174
Kale, Pear & Grapefruit Juice 174
Green Veggies & Fruit Juice 175
Kale, Spinach, Pear & Fennel Juice 175
Apple, Celery & Herbs Juice 176
Apple, Celery & Cucumber Juice 176
Pear & Kiwi Juice 177
Kale, Cucumber & Parsley Juice 177
Greens, Celery & Carrot Juice 178
Kale & Celery Juice 178

Conclusion 179
Index of Ingredients 180

Special Bonus!

Want This Bonus Challenge + Book for FREE?

Get **FREE**, unlimited access to it and all of my new books by joining the Fan Base!

Scan W/ Your Camera To Join!

Before we get started, I'd like to offer you this gift. It's my way of saying thank you for spending time with me in this book. Your gift is a special report titled *"The 30-Day Plant-Based Challenge."* As a bonus, you will also receive *"The Plant-Based Nutrient Cheat Sheet & Micronutrient Guide."* This is a 30-day challenge, and an easy-to-use guide that pulls together tons of analysis and fun activates you can enjoy doing every day. This guide will help you understand what exactly could be missing in your plant-based diet to achieve your health and fitness dreams. This guide will make sure you are eating clean and making sure you are getting all the nutrients you need daily to help you along with whatever fitness dreams you have. Whether you want to lose weight, burn fat, build lean muscle, or even bump up your confidence, this challenge and guide are just for you.

Paulgreencookbook.com

This 2 in 1 gift includes:

- ✓ Complete 30 days of daily plant-based fun and activities you will love
- ✓ 80+ detailed micronutrient information of the most common plant-based foods at your fingertips
- ✓ Basic Beginner steps to cover all the basic information you need to hop into the plant-based lifestyle
- ✓ The micronutrient guide will provide you with essential information about the body's vitamin and mineral requirements
- ✓ The cheat sheet guide will make your transition to a whole foods plant-based diet very simple

I'm willing to bet you'll find at least a few ideas, tools and meals covered in this gift that will surprise and help you. This guide will set you up for success and is a proven system when starting your plant-based journey. With this guide, you will be armed with the info & focus you need. You will be giving your body nutritious fuel and enjoy eating plant-based foods. With downloading this guide, you're taking a solid step to the path of your health and fitness dreams.

How can you obtain a copy of **The 30-Day Plant-Based Challenge** and the **Plant-Based Nutrient Cheat Sheet & Micronutrient Guide?** It's simple. Visit paulgreencookbook.com and sign up for my email list (or simply click the link above). You'll receive immediate access to the guides in PDF format. You can read it online, download it or print it out. Everything you need to get started and stay on your plant-based journey is included when you sign up for my email list.

Being on my email list also means you'll be the first to know when I release a new book. I plan to release my books at a steep discount (or even for free). By signing up for my email list, you'll get an early notification.

If you don't want to join my list, that's fine. This just means I need to earn your trust. With this in mind, I think you will love the information I've included in the ultimate guide. More specifically, I think you will love what it can do for your life.

Without further ado, let's jump into this book.

Join The Plant-Based Health, Fitness, And Nutrition Facebook Group

Looking for a community of like minded individuals who love all things plant base, working out, fitness, nutrition and health? If so, then check out my Facebook community: The Plant-Based, Health, Fitness and Nutrition Community.

This is an amazing group of plant-based health enthusiast who focus on getting results with their lives. Here you can discover simple strategies along your health journey, build powerful habits and relationships, find accountability partners, and ask questions about your struggles. I also host free book giveaways and share other helpful free resources that will be the key to reaching your health and fitness goals as fast as possible. If you want to "level up" in your health and fitness journey then this is the place to be.

**Just scan the QR code below
to join The Plant-Based, Health, Fitness and Nutrition Community**

Attention
Do Not Turn The Page Until You Have Read Everything Below

Scan the QR code below to receive the ebook version of this cookbook that includes all the pictures of each receipe!

Scan W/ Camera Now!

Due to printing costs, we are not able to provide you with a print book with colors and pictures. Instead, I have provided you the ebook version for you to download completely for free with the full cookbook for your ultimate plant-based experience. I want my book to be easily accessible for everyone in the world and since we are a small publishing company, this is the best we can offer to still keep the price for you as low as possible. Hopefully, in the near future, we would like to change this by offering the best quality of books in the world for the lowest prices. Thank you for your understanding and we greatly appreciate your support.

Introduction

Every year, 11 million people lose their lives worldwide because of unhealthy dietary practices and poor lifestyles. Nutrition is a significant determinant of living a quality life. The steep rise in life-threatening chronic diseases in this age is mainly because of the lack of a nutritious and balanced diet in our lives. The situation seems alarming, with no immediate solution! The trends, however, can be reversed or prevented in the future to come, by choosing a healthier lifestyle and eating nutrient-dense foods with a mix of macro, micro, and phytonutrients. The plant-based lifestyle has emerged as the right fix for this ongoing health crisis; it recommends much-needed dietary changes. Nutritional sciences highly value plant-based food due to its recorded health benefits. And if you too love your health, then this cookbook is the perfect fit for you!

Following a health-oriented diet plan is difficult, especially when there are so many temptations out there with limited choices to eat healthy. It is almost impossible to eat out from my personal experience without having to compromise on your diet plan. Restaurants which offer a vegetarian menu are rare to find, and the dieters are then left with no other choice but to eat salads and pasta. The struggle gets real when you eat at your friend's place, and if you show up without having your plant-based food backup, then you will be left to eat only drinks and chips. The smart choice is to rely on your homemade plant-based food. This cookbook can offer you all your favorite delights in one place.

Getting onto the plant-based dietary approach is not easy for most dieters, as the recipes available in most of the cookbooks are either too complex or too fancy to try on a daily basis. Every beginner needs delicious yet simple and easy recipes to begin incorporating all the plant-based ingredients into their diet without feeling the urge to quit. I like the recipes I am sharing in this cookbook because they are relatively simple and easy for all, especially for a novice cook.

Plant-based diet aids in the reversing of most chronic diseases. Health experts and doctors recommend this diet to those suffering from high blood pressure, cancer, and high cholesterol. By strictly following this approach, most dieters get rid of their medications and side effects. Here comes a fix to counter all your health problems! This whole food plant-based cookbook is written for all my fellow health-enthusiasts! There are 200 recipes in this comprehensive book that provides you with a world full of options to make your plant-based menu more diverse and flavorsome. Eating healthy and delicious smoothies and juices is now possible with my plant-based recipe collection.

This cookbook is written to introduce all the newbies to the plant-based diet and ease out their transition to this new lifestyle. All the recipes are carefully crafted with common ingredients mostly found in our homes or grocery stores. A picture of the finished meals accompanies each recipe to serve as your visual guide to compare the results of what you cooked and what you were supposed to cook.

Also, all the recipes in this book are provided with a complete nutritional profile, making it easier for you to keep track of your daily caloric intake. Lastly, all the ingredients from the recipes are listed in an organized index, given at the end of the book, to help you find a recipe with any particular ingredient.

Switching to a new diet plan is always overwhelming. Only a good understanding of the diet can help a beginner garner a dietary approach's actual benefits.

When I started my plant-based diet journey, there were lots of challenges that came along the way- the first being ignorance and lack of awareness. During my 20s, I was never really a health-enthusiast; eating healthy was never my priority. Weight gain came next. As soon as I crossed 30, I experienced the effects of my unhealthy food choices on my physical health. Obesity, high blood pressure, and high cholesterol became my reality. The medication worked, but that was not a permanent fix. These health conditions would have only gotten worse if my doctor had not suggested me the plant-based diet. This evoked my interest, and from that day onward, I extensively studied this concept. It took a certificate in Plant-based nutrition for me to finally acknowledge the importance of a plant-based lifestyle. Soon I turned to this diet and lost as much as 30 pounds, and I never looked back. After two years, my blood cholesterol dropped to normal levels, and I finally got rid of my medications. My insulin sensitivity improved, and it has been six years since, and I am still sticking to this dietary regime. I never felt this healthy and active ever in my life.

From my own struggles, I learned that it is essential to have complete knowledge and understanding of a diet to harness its real benefits. I was lucky that I had the resources to study plant-based nutrition myself; however, not everyone can afford to do so! So, I wrote this cookbook to compile the best plant-based recipes I tried and tested and found most useful for all the plant-based diet beginners.

So, if you value your health or you're suffering from chronic diseases, then switching to the plant-based diet will help. This cookbook is your calling to a healthy lifestyle. It is here to ease this transition for you with its wide variety of delicious plant-based smoothie and juice recipes- all categorized into chapters to meet your daily needs. Give it a read, pick out your favorite plant-based smoothie and juices, and see your health improve in no time!

CHAPTER 01
THE PLANT-BASED SMOOTHIE AND JUICE MAGIC

Smoothies and juices serve various purposes in a diet plan. They can be served in the morning or between two meals since they are light and easy to digest. Instead of having a solid meal continuously throughout the day, break the routine and try something refreshing and quick to make. When you make these smoothies and juices, use dairy-free plant-based ingredients. You can ensure you are getting high intake of fibers, lots of vitamins, and minerals. That's how the magic of the plant-based smoothies and juices work.

Chapter 1: The Plant-Based Smoothie and Juice Magic

Benefits of A Smoothie and Juicing Lifestyle

We all know smoothies and fresh homemade juices are health transforming magical drinks, and there is no doubt in their effectiveness. But most importantly, it is about the type and ingredients in the smoothies, which make them replenishing and nourishing. A healthy lifestyle is a must to reap the full benefits of these smoothies.

Nutritionists claim smoothies prepared out of clean vegetables and fruits contain all the nutrients heavily packed inside, and no energy and nutrients are lost during the preparation. Even fibers remain intact, which later supports our digestive system and accelerates our metabolism. From liver to spleen, and intestines, everything functions more effectively when you are on a smoothie diet. Due to fresh and rich ingredients, a smoothie can have a full stomach feeling without adding too many calories, fats, and carbs to your diet. Its detoxifying properties are another reason doctors recommend some heart and cancer patients drink smoothies regularly for better health.

Detoxification of the Body

The nutritional content used to make smoothies and juices like lime, lemon, berries, citrus fruits, spinach, mint, kale, broccoli, avocados, etc., all contain powerful antioxidants, and when they enter our bloodstream, they actively remove all the radicals, toxins, and cell debris. This process of detoxification keeps our minds fresh and our metabolism active (Maeda, 2013). That is why it is recommended to have a glass of smoothie right at the beginning of the day and as your breakfast. It will give you a boost in energy for the day and remove the metabolic waste over the day. Remember, only regular use can help you achieve the desired effects.

Sources of Phytonutrients

Phytochemicals and nutrients improve the internal body condition, and they can prevent the contraction of many harmful diseases. They are natural compounds that plants produce through photosynthesis. Most fruits contain these phytonutrients like bananas, mango, kiwi, berries, etc. Diana Dyer, a dietician and a three time cancer survivor, believes these fruits, combined with flaxseeds, nuts, carrots, etc., can make the best disease-preventing smoothies (Getz, 2009).

Antioxidants and Anti-inflammatory

All phytonutrients have two properties in common; they all are powerful antioxidants and anti-inflammatory in nature. There are five thousand different phytonutrients that are present in plants. The most commonly found phytonutrients include carotenoids, flavonoids, resveratrol, ellagic acid, phytoestrogens, and glucosinolates. They strengthen our immune system, eliminate toxins, and prevents cancer. Each phytonutrient works differently to carry out specific changes in the body. Vegetables like broccoli, cabbage, bok choy, etc., contain high doses of glucosinolates, whereas green tea is a good source of flavonoids. Resveratrol, and ellagic acid, are mostly found in berries and nuts (Islam et al., 2014).

Boosts Energy

The smoothies suggested in this cookbook are full of clean energy in complex carbohydrates, fats, fibers, minerals, and proteins. A glass of a smoothie is enough to boost your energy levels (Jam, 2019).

Improves Mental Health

The antioxidant that is chiefly present in these smoothies has amazing results on a person's cognitive abilities. These antioxidants help remove all the toxins and debris from your brain cells and the nutrients nourish the cells to work optimally.

Gives Better Sleep

Fruits and green vegetables contain phytonutrients that have healing properties. People who suffer from insomnia or restlessness can use these green smoothies to have a good nights sleep. The phytonutrients improve the production and transmission of the neurotransmitters essential for sleep.

Fights Unwanted Cravings

A sugar and carb-rich diet can help induce cravings for unhealthy food. By replacing such food with green, fruity smoothies, a person can also fight against those cravings. Over 10 days, the body embraces this change in diet and eventually helps reduce those cravings.

Improves Digestion

Imagine having lots of greens every day! It is equally refreshing for your gut as it is for our mood. Green leafy vegetables are full of fibers that help bowel movements and keeps the digestive system healthy and active. A smoothie or juice is quickly digested, and the nutrients are then readily absorbed.

Reduces Daily Bloating

The green smoothie recipes also helps reduce bloating since it is free from all such ingredients that cause bloating. It keeps the gut healthy and nourishes our gut microbiome.

Better Physical Health

Smoothies have radicalizing effects on our mind and body, and that's not just me claiming this. Dr. Mark Hyman, Dr. Kristi Funk, Elaine Magee, and many others share the same view. These are not written claims, but smoothies' effects are proven over time in reducing obesity, losing weight, improving the gut condition, maintaining cholesterol levels, detoxification, and preventing cancer. Perhaps when it comes to health, smoothies serve as a magic potion with varying ingredients with your favorite flavors.

Source of Antioxidants

Green smoothies swiftly detoxify the body from harmful radicals. The fibrous leafy greens and citrus fruits are paired together to give a potion with loads of antioxidants. These smoothies are also carb-free, which makes their content suitable for different diets.

Aids Weight Loss

Weight loss is another major objective of having smoothies in our diet. A single glass of a smoothie can be as filling as any other snack, but it is low on calories and carbs. No fats and no extra carbs, all-natural ingredients are added to the mixture, which does not let any fat accumulate in the body and prevents inflammation in the body. Any smoothie prepared for weight loss should not be mixed with sugars or similar ingredients.

Helps Cancer Prevention

Cancer prevention is another known impact of smoothies by nutritionists and doctors. Anti-cancer smoothies are prepared with plant-based ingredients which can replenish brain and skin cells. Patients on chemotherapies and high-dose medications need this support to gain a boost in energy. Free radicals which can otherwise cause cell mutation are also actively removed from the body through the agents found in cleansing smoothies. They directly work on our liver to boost its functionality and cleanse the blood flowing in and out of it more effectively (B.S 2012).

Fights Inflammation

Inflammation is usually caused by the oxidants, toxins, and free radicals circulating in our blood. These toxins can trigger the body's immune system, which results in inflammation in different parts of the body, both at the cellular or organ level. Smoothies can reduce this inflammation by providing antioxidants that remove all the toxins from the blood.

Chapter 1: The Plant-Based Smoothie and Juice Magic

Introduce Healthy Ingredients	According to health experts, an average adult should consume 400grams of fruits and vegetables per day. But in today's lifestyle, we are more dependent on processed and fast food, and the fresh fruit and vegetable levels in our diets are low. Smoothies can help you maintain your fruit and vegetable intake without putting in much effort in cooking and preparation. You have the choice to add many healthy ingredients to meet your nutritional needs.
Speeds Up Metabolism	Phytonutrients are plant-sourced micronutrients commonly present in leafy green vegetables. These phytonutrients can regulate the hormones and enzymes produced in the body, help remove bad cholesterol, prevents cardiac diseases, causes weight loss, and boost metabolic rates. These phytonutrients rarely are consumed through a regular diet, but when vegetables are blended well with fruits, more phytonutrients are added to your diet. Thus, smoothies, through their high phytonutrient content, can help prevent various diseases.
Reduces Blood Cholesterol	The antioxidants and phytonutrients present in smoothies removes blood cholesterol from the body. They help your body to process these low-density lipoproteins and regulate hormones and enzymes that remove these molecules from the blood and cleanse them.
Higher Fiber Consumption	On average, a human adult must consume 25-38 grams of fiber per day. But the standard American diet we consume does not offer that much fiber. Smoothies are a rich source of fiber. You can drastically increase your fiber intake to help meet your daily requirements.

Chapter 1: The Plant-Based Smoothie and Juice Magic

Juicing Vs. Smoothies

Let's start with the concept of juicing to better understand the pros and cons of both concepts. Juicing is primarily the extraction of juices out of the chosen produce, whether they are fruits or vegetables. When you juice, you remove all the fiber and are left with the juice of the vegetable or fruit. Juices have a lighter consistency and are also low in calories. They also have a higher proportion of nutrients other than fiber. Juices are refreshing, and they cannot be used to replace a meal because they lack macronutrients like proteins and fats.

Smoothies are prepared using the blending process. When blending, you add and mix all the parts of the vegetable or fruit without leaving any residue or pulp behind. Due to blending, all the fiber-rich content of the fruit and vegetable become part of the drink, and you get to drink it all in a single gulp. Thus, smoothies can be naturally high caloric drinks. They are richer in nutritional content, and they can easily replace a full meal if prepared using extra proteins and superfoods.

Chapter 1: The Plant-Based Smoothie and Juice Magic

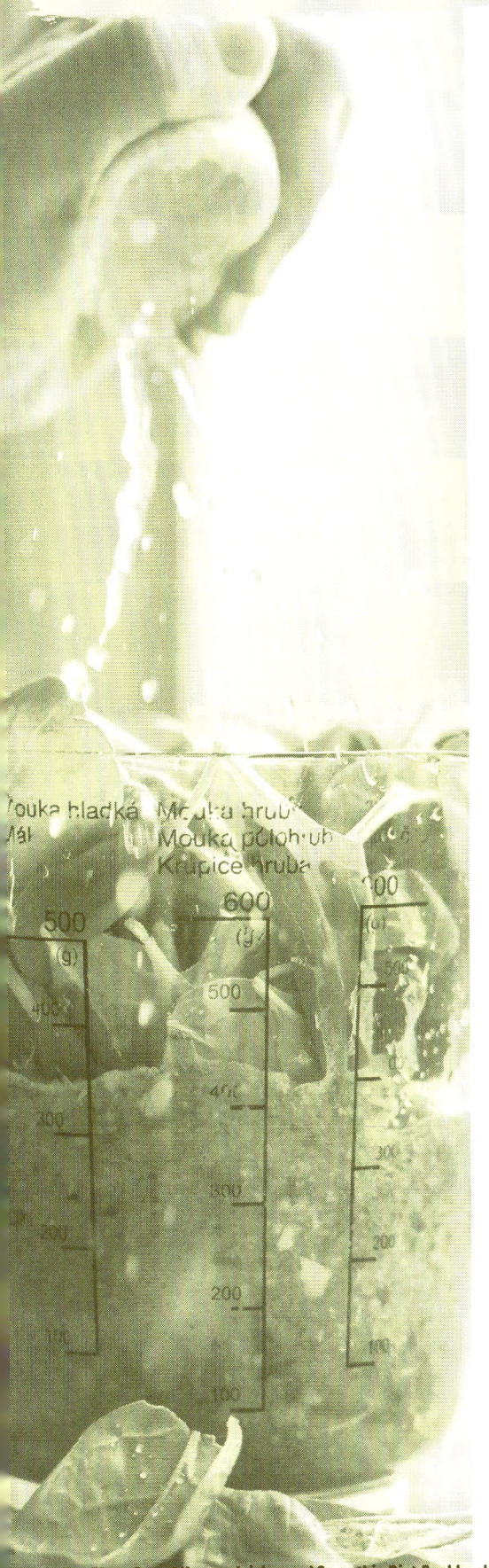

Blending and Juicing Rules to Follow

Depending on the type of smoothie you are looking to have, select the appropriate ingredients and benefits of them. It is best to prepare it for a single serving since storing it can ruin the fresh taste, flavor, and nutrients of a smoothie or juice. Always select a balancing combination; if you choose green vegetables, add a sweetening fruit to diffuse the taste and create a mild flavor. Similarly, we can add extras like agave, dates, dark chocolate, cacao powder for extra flavor.

Most smoothies require no cooking, and ingredients are directly put together. Prepare them by peeling, trimming, coring, or deseeding beforehand. It is better to chop them roughly and put them together in a blender of your choice. If it is brewed coffee or tea liquid, then prepare them by conventional methods, allow them to cool then add to the blender.

Now that everything is in place, it's about time to give it a pulse and blend the ingredients until they form a nice and smooth consistency. Some granules are expected if there are seeds and nuts used in the recipe. Give 2-3 three pulses with a 30 seconds gap between to mix all the ingredients together thoroughly or blend until you have the desired consistency and texture.

Pour your smoothie into serving glasses or cups of choice. A good garnish is essential for every smoothie and makes it taste even more delicious. Try some fruit slices, shredded coconut, fruit cubes, or crushed nuts on top of each serving or use them in combination, then serve right away.

How to Get The Most Benefits Out of Juicing or Blending

By making plant-based, dairy-free, and vegan smoothies and juices, you can get the most benefits out of them by:

- Wash all the produce thoroughly and use fresh ingredients.

- It is best to drink smoothies and juices when they are fresh. When left to time and air, these drinks oxidized and spoil, so either drink immediately or store in the refrigerator.

- Do not blend fruit with vegetables without knowing about the taste of their blend. Some veggies are bitter, and they don't go with all fruits. For instance, broccoli, beetroots, and carrots make a super starchy combination with other fruits.

- Invest in good quality juicers and blenders to get the best drinks in a short amount of time. Besides the essential equipment, you will also need side tools like a knife, peeler, corer, and grater to prepare the veggies and fruits.

Going Dairy Free

Dairy includes milk and all the products derived from it like yogurt, cream, cream cheese, butter, cheese, etc. When you say dairy free, you mean to avoid using all such ingredients while making these smoothies and juices. Removing dairy from your recipes makes them plant-based and healthy for people who can not eat dairy for various reasons.

 ### The Truth About Dairy

For years, we have been thinking of animal-sourced food, especially dairy products, as essential for good health. But recent research has shown just the opposite scenario, as the fats and carbs present in milk can elevate the blood cholesterols, and the enzymes and nutrients present in dairy can upset the digestive and endocrine system of your body.

 ### Benefits of Going Dairy Free

By making smoothies and juices dairy free, you can harness these known benefits:

- Dairy free smoothies and juices are great for achieving weight loss. Dairy products are rich in fats and some carbs, which can lead to weight gain.

- Dairy free drinks are also great for those who are lactose intolerant.

- Without any dairy products, smoothies and juices can be easily digested as they are no complex nutrients present that our stomachs cannot digest easily.

- Dairy products may contain hormones and enzymes which can interact with our metabolism and cause health problems. Going dairy free prevents that.

CHAPTER 02

INGREDIENTS TO A HEALTHIER YOU

Living on smoothies and juices is of no benefit to your body if you are not choosing healthy ingredients every time. This new lifestyle can only work out for you, if you eat and prepare more organic plant-based ingredients and avoid dairy and other processed items by adding them into your smoothies and juices. In this section, you can find all the healtheist ingredients that are most suitable for smoothie and juice making.

Top 8 Greens for Your Smoothies

Green smoothies are known for their rich nutritional content, and those that are made out of leafy green vegetables are packed with phytonutrients. These smoothies are more effective for weight loss. Kale, spinach, parsley, celery, coriander, etc., are usually added to these smoothies along with water or a nut milk base.

Kale
Kale is full of important nutrients like potassium, protein, iron, vitamins A, C, and B6, calcium, and many more.

Arugula
This green vegetable is packed with many nutrients like fiber, calcium, protein, and phytochemicals, including beta-carotene.

Swiss Chard
Chard is an excellent source of vitamins like vitamin A, C, and K, along with iron, calcium, and other micronutrients.

Broccoli
The bitter flavored broccoli comes with its own nutritional benefits as it contains lots of fiber and vitamins C, A, and K.

Celery
Celery also has many health benefits, like regulating the body's alkaline levels and reducing inflammation while improving digestion.

Parsley
This powerful herb is loaded with iron and vitamins A, C, and K, along with several antioxidants.

Spinach
Spinach leaves are loaded with iron and antioxidants, which boosts your immune system and relieves inflammation. These vegetables can be consumed in everyday meals or in drinks and beverages.

Chinese Cabbage or Bok Choy
It is a low caloric green vegetable, and it is packed with dietary fiber, protein, and vitamins K and C

Best Vegetables for Your Smoothies

Vegetables make your smoothies more nutritious and nourishing. You can add all sorts of vegetables to your smoothies. Here are some commonly used ones:

Zucchini

It is a vitamin-packed vegetable that is very low in calories but high in water content, which makes it an excellent fit for a healthy smoothie.

Pumpkin

Pumpkin smoothies make a nice serving. Pumpkins have a mildly sweet taste, and they are loaded with minerals, fibers, and vitamins.

Cucumber

Beta carotene is present in cucumbers, and it helps with the immune system, health of the skin and eyes and helps prevent cancer.

Beetroot

Beetroot contains antioxidants, fiber, and vitamin C, which boosts the immune system. It also contains folate and manganese, which help improve brain activity, the nervous system, and the body's endocrine system.

Carrot

Carrots are loaded with vitamins and minerals, including potassium, fiber, vitamin C, vitamin A, iron, beta-carotene, copper, and folate.

Tomato

Tomatoes are a good source of vitamins C and A, along with folate, fibers, and lycopene. They can help promote eye health, fight diabetes, and keeps your skin look younger.

Best Medical Herbs You Can Add to Smoothies

Herbs are your extra tickets to good health. They are not used in large amounts, but the micronutrients present in them are highly beneficial for your body and mind.

Basil

Basil has a warm taste that can boost the flavor of all your green smoothies and help improve the function of your kidneys.

Parsley

Parsley works by assisting the bladder, kidneys, liver and filters and detoxifies the blood.

Cilantro

Cilantro is known for a variety of nutrients; one of the incredible health benefits of cilantro is that it is detoxifying and helps your body get rid of radicals.

Cinnamon

Cinnamon is a good immunity booster as it has both calcium and iron. It has a warming taste and smell that gives smoothies great flavor.

Mint

Mint is known for improving digestion, reducing cramping, constipation, or bloating. Mint is an instant reliever for all your stomach problems.

Turmeric

Turmeric is a commonly used Indian spice added to food for its endless health benefits. The yellow color spice can make your drink super healthy and delicious. Turmeric also contains curcumin, an anti-inflammatory compound, and research has suggested that turmeric can also help relieve soreness or joint pain.

Chapter 2: Ingredients to a Healthier You

Top Fruits for Your Smoothies

Some of the most commonly used and highly nutritious fruits you can always add to your smoothies include:

Citrus Fruits

Citrus fruits are a rich source of Vitamin C, which plays a vital role in collagen formation and absorption of calcium in the body. Adding citrus juice to your smoothies also extends their shelf life.

- Lemon
- Limes
- Oranges

Avocados and Coconut

Both avocados and coconuts are low in carbs, but they both contain healing properties. They are rich in antioxidants, which can reduce inflammation. Coconut water and its flesh, milk, and cream are excellent for an anti-inflammatory diet.

Chapter 2: Ingredients to a Healthier You

Berries

Berries belong to that group of food that contains a lot of antioxidants. They also keep your carb and caloric intake in control. Among all the fruits, berries are most recommended for an anti-inflammatory diet. They can be added to desserts or snacks and smoothies. Daily use of berries can even prevent the usual puffiness of the face and hands.

- Blackberries
- Blueberries
- Raspberries
- Strawberries
- Cherries
- Cranberries

Grapes

The skin of grapes contains resveratrol, which is a phytonutrient, and it is excellent in boosting the immune system, and it also prevents prostate cancer and inflammation. The dark red color of these grapes is because of the presence of resveratrol in them.

Tropical Fruits

These fruits are loaded with more liquid and fewer calories. By adding tropical fruits to your smoothies, you can make your smoothies more hydrating and nourishing for your cells.

- Kiwi
- Mango
- Melon
- Pineapple

Other Fruits

Other fruits you can add to the smoothies and increase their nutritional value include:

- Apple
- Apricot
- Bananas
- Figs
- Peach
- Pomegranate
- Pears

Best Superfoods, Seeds, and Powders

These smoothies are extremely healthy and helpful for those looking for a protein-rich diet and working hard to develop strong and healthy muscles. You can increase the protein content of your smoothies by adding more nuts, seeds, and protein powder.

 **Acai**	This grape-like berry fruit is known for its nutritional benefits. It has anti-cancerous properties, and these berries are also good for heart health and cognitive function.
 **Cacao**	Cacao powder or cocoa powder are two words interchangeably used, but know that cacao is the raw, less-processed variety of cocoa, and due to this minimal processing, cacao is rich in flavonoids. These have been shown to boost blood flow to the brain. Cacao also has anti-inflammatory properties.
 **Camu Camu Powder**	The pale orange powder, Camu Camu, is packed with vitamin C. A single teaspoon of Camu Camu can serve 2,400 milligrams of Vitamin C per serving, which is about 30 times more than an orange. Vitamin C is excellent and healthy for your skin and helps fight against skin damage caused by UV rays coming from the sun. It also boosts the production of skin-smoothing collagen.
 **Chia Seeds**	Like hemp seeds, these tiny seeds are also packed with proteins, omega-3s, and fiber. A 2-tablespoon serving can provide 6 grams of protein, 10 grams of fiber, and 5 grams of omega 3s. They are also suitable for meeting your nutritional needs for minerals like iron and magnesium.

 **Chlorella**	Chlorella is best known for improving your immune system and digestive system. It can also help detoxify the body.
 **Goji Berries**	These red-orange berries will add some sweetness to a smoothie, and they also contain several nutrients. They are packed with zeaxanthin, which is an antioxidant commonly known to improve eyesight and health. Goji berries come with a good amount of fiber, about 2 ½ grams per 2 tablespoons of serving.
 **Ground Flaxseeds**	Flaxseeds are fiber-rich seeds mostly added to your smoothies to give you both the taste, texture, and extra nutritional value to your smoothies.
 **Hemp Seeds**	Go for these little seeds to add a protein boost to your everyday smoothie recipes. A 3-tablespoon serving of hemp seeds can add 10 grams of protein to each serving, which is more than enough to meet your protein needs. In this serving, you can also get 10 grams of omega-3 fatty acids, which can support your heart and brain health.
 **Maca**	This cream-colored powder has been used for a long time to regulate hormones, boost energy, treat anxiety and depression, and help with focus. Maca can provide you with a great number of nutrients like iron and Vitamin C.

Chapter 2: Ingredients to a Healthier You

 **Matcha**	If you often visit a coffee shop, then you must be familiar with matcha green powder. Matcha powder is a concentrated form of green tea, and it is packed with antioxidants like ECGC, which has been used to prevent tumor formation in human cells and reduces the risk for certain types of cancers. Studies have revealed that it has strong anti-infective properties, and it helps boost metabolism in the body.
 **Maqui**	It is a dark purple powder, which provides more antioxidants than other fruits like blueberries, acai berries, pomegranates, or blackberries. Maqui is rich in anthocyanins, which is a family of phytonutrients that have been seen to have a preventive effect against heart problems and cancer formation. It might help your strength to fight against a common cold or flu; a few pieces of evidence suggest that anthocyanins also have antimicrobial properties.
 **Mushroom Powders**	Mushroom powders improve your immune system, alleviate stress, enhance sleep quality, and reduce fatigue. People can take a mushroom powder to fight against health conditions like high blood pressure and high blood cholesterol.
 **Raw Walnuts**	Walnuts are loaded with minerals, essential oils, and vitamins. Having walnuts in the smoothies can help improve your brain function.
 **Spirulina**	Spirulina contains a plant-based protein called phycocyanin. It also contains anti-inflammatory, pain-relief, antioxidant, and brain-protective properties.

Chapter 2: Ingredients to a Healthier You

Best Vegan Protein Powders for Smoothies

Most protein-based smoothies call for protein powders. On a plant-based diet, you can not just get any protein powder available in the market. You must find only those which are sourced from plants. Some of the commonly available, good quality protein powders include:

- Tone It Up Plant-Based Protein Powder
- Orgain Organic Plant-Based Protein Powder
- KOS Organic Plant-Based Vegan Protein Powder
- Garden of Life Raw Organic Protein
- Your Super Skinny Protein Mix
- Nuzest Clean Lean Protein
- Vega One All-In-One Plant-Based Protein Powder
- Sakara Life Source Super Powder
- Optimum Nutrition Gold Standard 100% Organic Plant-Based Protein Powder
- Aloha Organic Protein Powder
- Designer Protein Essential 10 100% Plant-Based Meal Replacement
- Body Logix Vegan Protein
- Plant Protein
- SunWarrior Plant-Based Vegan Protein Blend
- BN Labs Organic Vegan Protein Powder

Best Liquid Bases for Your Smoothies

For smoothies, you can add known plant-based liquid bases, like:

Filtered Water

Water is the zero-caloric liquid base, so it is best to make low-caloric and low-carb smoothies.

Coconut Water

Coconut water is another way to add a refreshing taste to the smoothie without adding many calories.

Fresh Juice

Any juice extract from fruit like orange or pineapple juice can also be a liquid-based for a plant-based smoothie.

Almond Milk

It is most commonly used and prescribed as non-dairy milk, which can be used in all sorts of smoothies, cakes, confectioneries, cookies, and mousses.

Coconut Milk

Obtained from fresh coconut flesh, this form of milk is the second most used non-dairy product used in all low-carb meals and smoothies.

Rice Milk

Rice milk is another non-dairy option to go for. It has a light consistency and a mild taste. However, rice milk is not low in carbs.

Oat Milk

Oat milk is excellent for making all sorts of smoothies. It is a rich source of proteins and minerals.

Green Tea

Green tea is packed with lots of phytonutrients and antioxidants; adding green tea as a base will make your smoothies super healthy and anti-inflammatory.

Things Not to Add to Your Smoothies

Do you want to harness the amazing benefits of the plant-based smoothie and juicing lifestyle? Well, you must say goodbye to these ingredients as they do not go with a healthy plant-based lifestyle.

 Sugar-sweetened fruit juice or concentrate

Sugar and sweeteners like honey, maple syrup, molasses, etc., may add the desired sweetness to the smoothie, but when you overdo the quantity of sugar in a smoothie, it can drastically increase its sugar value which are hazardous for health. If you are having a smoothie with lots of fruits then you are already getting enough sugar from them.

 Flavored yogurt

Yogurt contains artificial flavors, sweeteners, and chemicals which are not suitable for this diet and the lifestyle, so it must be avoided.

 Flavored kefir

Flavored kefir is also packed with chemicals and preservatives, which is not suitable for this diet plan.

 Whipped cream

Whipped cream is dairy, so it is not appropriate for a plant-based diet.

 Ice cream

Ice cream is made out of dairy milk which is not the right option to consume on a plant-based diet.

 Sorbet

Sorbet available in the market usually have chemicals, artificial flavors, and preservatives, hence not good for this diet.

 Sherbet

Sherbet is the artificially flavored processed juices that are not good for health. They are high in calories, so they must be avoided.

 Chocolate syrup

Market-bought chocolate syrup is packed with sugar and artificial flavors, so it must be avoided.

 Milk

Milk is dairy and packed with artificial sweeteners; both of these qualities make this milk not suitable for this diet.

 Canned fruit in syrup

Canned fruit contains artificial flavors, sweeteners, and chemicals which are not suitable for this diet and the lifestyle, so it must be avoided.

Chapter 2: Ingredients to a Healthier You

Top Vegetables for Juicing

Vegetable juices are packed with phytonutrients, minerals, fibers, and vitamins. The great thing about these vegetables is that they are low in calories and low in carbs. You can try these commonly known vegetables to extract their refreshing juices:

- Beets
- Broccoli
- Cabbage
- Carrots
- Celery
- Cucumbers

- Kale
- Parsley
- Spinach
- Swiss Chard
- Tomatoes
- Wheatgrass

Top Fruits for Juicing

Most fruits are loaded with sap and juices, which are naturally sweet and refreshing. Their juices contain natural sweeteners, which are not harmful to your health. They are healthy for the mind, body, and skin due to all the antioxidants and enzymes they contain. Here are some juicy fruits that you can always choose for juicing:

- Apples
- Blueberries
- Cranberries
- Grapefruits
- Grapes
- Lemons

- Mangos
- Oranges
- Peaches
- Pineapples
- Pomegranates

Herbs, Spices, Mix-Ins

Adding herbs and spices to your juices enhances the taste and improves the nutritional value of juices. Here are some herbs and spices that you can add to a juice:

- Arugula
- Basil
- Chamomile
- Cilantro
- Cinnamon
- Dandelion
- Fennel
- Fenugreek
- Garlic
- Ginger
- Jalapeno
- Milk Thistle
- Mint
- Nettle
- Parsley
- Purslane

How to Wash Your Produce

Fresh leafy green vegetables can be washed under running water in a colander, then leave them out for 2 minutes until the water is drained out. Some fruits and veggies like melons, cucumber, potatoes, and citrus fruits need some scrubbing before washing. For that, you can use a scrub brush to scrape off the dirt lightly. Once scrubbed, you can then rinse these ingredients underwater. Use a colander to wash the bunched produce like radishes, and grapes, etc. Make sure not to wash the produce with any detergent, soap, or commercial chemicals.

How to Use A Scrub Brush?

This brush is made out of nylon bristles which can lightly scrape off the dirt and microbes from the surface of your fruits and vegetables. To use this brush, lightly run its bristles over the veggies and fruits in one direction, from top to bottom and then rinse underwater.

How to Prepare Your Produce

You can prepare each fruit and vegetable according to its use in a juice and smoothie. Here are some basic ingredients with their method of preparations:

Apples

Apples can be used in a variety of ways, whole, unpeeled, peeled, and diced. Make sure to core the apple and take out the seeds.

Beets

The top and end of the beets are chopped off, then they are peeled and diced before adding to a smoothie or juice.

Berries

Berries can be added in a variety of ways. Use fresh berries.

Carrots

Carrots are chopped off from top and bottom. Peel or wash the dirt off the carrots, then either blend it directly or parboil it first before juicing if you desire. You can also juice them directly as well.

Chapter 2: Ingredients to a Healthier You

Cucumbers

Cucumbers must be cleaned with an antimicrobial wash to remove all the wax. Peel them and then transfer them to the juicer or blender.

Leafy Vegetables

They are the easiest to prepare. Simply wash and drain them, then cut off the stem and hard ribs from the center.

Lemons and Limes

Both the peels and juice of citrus fruit are used in smoothies and juices. For peel, use a grater, and for juicing, simply only put the fruit in the juicer and not the peels. Make sure you take out all the seeds before hand.

Mangos and Papayas

Remove the peel and pit of the mangos and seeds from papaya before adding their flesh to the juicer or blender.

Melons

Watermelons are only peeled, and seeds should be removed before juicing. For cantaloupe and honeydew, you can remove the seeds to avoid the bitter flavor.

Oranges and Grapefruits

Cut these fruits, juice their flesh and take out the seeds.

Pineapples

Cut the green crown from the top of the pineapple and remove the core from the center, then use the flesh after cutting it into quarters.

Passion Fruit

Cut the fruit in half and scoop out the flesh using a small ice cream scoop. For juicing, remove the seeds first, then once the fruit is juiced, you can add the seeds later if you desire.

What to Do with The Pulp After Juicing

Fruit and vegetable pulp are so dense in fiber that you can use this pulp for several other purposes:

1. You can add the leftover pulp to a smoothie to increase its fiber content.
2. This pulp can also be added to a soup to make it more dense, thick, and rich in fiber.
3. The pulp is great for making frozen popsicles. Blend it with ice, some liquid base, and freeze in the popsicle mold.
4. The pulp obtained from vegetables and fruits can be used to make vegetable broth.
5. Fruit pulp is excellent to add to a fruit tea. Cook the pulp with water and some whole spices and sweetener, then strain and serve.
6. You can always add the vegetable pulp to meals like mac and cheese or lasagna.
7. Fruit pulp is excellent for making fruit leathers.
8. Vegetable pulp can add great texture, flavor, nutrition, and moisture to the vegetable burgers and fritters.
9. Like fritters, the leftover pulp can also be added to baked goods like bread, cakes, muffins, granola bars, and cookies.
10. If you are making morning pancakes, you can always add vegetable or fruit pulp to the batter.
11. This pulp can always be dehydrated to make crackers. Spread the pulp in a thin layer in a baking sheet, dehydrate at low heat, and break into crackers.
12. The pulp is also a great addition to pizza crust.
13. Are you making a marmalade? Well, you can add the fruit pulp to it and make it tastier.
14. You can also make a crumble by mixing the pulp with some juice, oats, nuts, seeds, and spices.
15. Trail mix bars can also be made using this pulp and some dried fruits, nuts, and seeds.
16. Dehydrate and crush the pulp to make healthy breadcrumbs.
17. The fruit and vegetable pulp are also great to add to homemade skincare products like soap, maskers, and scrubs.
18. If you still do not want to use this pulp for yourself, you can always add it to your dog's food or make chicken's feed out of it.
19. You can also use it as compost for your garden as well.

CHAPTER 03

THE ESSENTIAL KITCHEN TOOLS FOR SMOOTHIES AND JUICES

Juicing and blending are impossible without proper tools and equipment. In this section, you can learn all about the essential equipment required for this lifestyle and how to use them.

Chapter 3: The Essential Kitchen Tools for Smoothies and Juices

Selecting the Best Blender

Are you still planning to get a blender? Well, you can consider all these options and see which one works best for you.

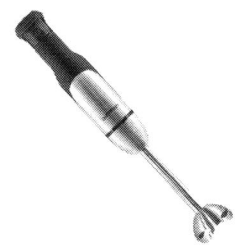

Hand or Immersion Blenders

These hand blenders allow you to puree many fruits, veggies and mix smoothie bases in a bowl. These blenders are great when making a smoothie bowl.

Countertop Blenders

These are standard kitchen blenders good for smoothies. You can buy a countertop blender with different sizes of jugs to meet all your serving size needs.

Mini Blenders

These blenders are designed for single servings, and they are great for people living in small spaces or people who are always traveling around. They are easy to use, chargeable, and portable. You can carry it around in a bag as well. Vitamix mini blenders are the best in this regard.

Commercial Blender

The Clean blend and Vitamix 5200 Blenders are popular high-powered professional blenders that are used professionally and can be great to have at home for smoothie making. Some other good options, include the Ninja and Blended blenders, which give professional results as well.

How to Choose the Best Blender for You

If you are planning to buy a blender and unable to decide which one to buy, then here are things that you need to think of first:

- First, start by estimating your budget. Some blenders can cost you up to $2,000. So even though these types of blenders are effective, not everyone can afford it. Think of your budget first, then look for a blender available in your set range.

- The next important thing is to think about is the investment of time. Not everyone can spare time every day to prepare the juices; they need to store and prep ahead.

- Cleaning up after smoothie making is also time-consuming, so add the cleanup time to your planning and then plan your schedule. If you can't do this daily, then come with a plan twice or three times per week.

- Then think about the shelf life of the smoothies you are planning to store. Weigh the pros and cons of daily blending and storing smoothies ahead.

- Think about the storage space in your kitchen and then plan to buy the right sized blender according to this space.

- Finally, think about the ingredients you will be blending and then buy the blender best suited for them.

Soaking Your Nuts, Oats, And Seeds

All grains, nuts, and seeds contain phytic acid, which is an enzyme inhibitor. It inhibits them from germinating when the environment is not suitable. When we eat grains, seeds, and nuts, the enzyme inhibitors may interact with other minerals and cause digestive irritation and nutritional deficiency. By soaking these foods in water, we activate the sprouting process, and thus the enzyme inhibitor is prevented from interacting with other nutrients. Once the nuts, seeds, and grains are soaked well, they are then rinsed and drained.

For Nuts/Seeds:

- 4 cups of raw nuts
- 1 tablespoon of sea salt
- Water

Add nuts to a bowl and pour enough water to cover them. Add salt and soak for 12 hours, then drain. Blend the nuts or seeds in the blender first until smooth before adding them into a smoothie.

For Grains:

- 1 cup of grain
- 1 tablespoon lemon juice or vinegar
- Water to cover

Add grains to a bowl and pour enough water to cover the grain. Add lemon juice and soak for 12 hours, then drain. Blend the grains in the blender first until smooth before adding them to the smoothie.

How to Store Your Smoothies

Smoothies do not have a long shelf life because they usually have a liquid base that can spoil easily if left without proper storage. Among the factors of spoilage, oxidization is another major cause.

Oxidization

Oxidization is a process in which the oxygen present in the air may interact with the contents of the smoothie and speeds up the breakdown of nutrients. No exposure to air can prevent this oxidization, and thus, the spoilage of the smoothie can also be prevented in this way.

Keeping It Fresh

However, you can always slow down the oxidization process and keep a smoothie fresh. Here are tricks that will help you do so:

- Adding antioxidants like citric acid to a smoothie can slow down this process. High amounts of citric acid are present in lemon, lime, or orange juices. So, add the juices or a piece of lemon or lime to the smoothie before storing.

- Always store a smoothie in a fully closed container so that no air can interact with the smoothie's content.

- Keep the smoothie in the refrigerator to slow down spoiling and the growth of bacteria.

- Even when kept in the refrigerator in a closed container, the shelf life of a smoothie is 24 hours. So do not store a smoothie longer than 24 hours.

Shelf Life

By following the above rules, you can only stretch the shelf life of a smoothie up to 24 hours in the refrigerator, and without a refrigerator, it is only 4 hours. After 24 hours, a smoothie can develop bacteria that can upset your stomach. So, it's not healthy to drink a smoothie that has been sitting for more than 24 hours.

Juicing Tools

Juicing becomes a lot more fun and less troublesome when you have the right tools at your disposal. Here are major tools that you will need while juicing produce:

 A Masticating Juicer

This can be any juicer of your choice. Since masticating juicers are economical and more efficient than centrifugal juicers, having them in the kitchen is a good option. These juicers give high yield and dry pulp.

 A Cleaning Brushes

A cleaning brush helps you clean the juicer and its components easily. Fruit and vegetable pulp usually gets stuck in the graters and gears of the juicer, and they can only be removed using a cleaning brush.

 A Sharp Knife

This knife will help you prepare fruits and vegetables for juicing. Some fruits and vegetables need to be peeled or cut into pieces before juicing. With a sharp knife, you can easily prepare them for this purpose.

 A Cutting Board

A cutting board is an everyday use kitchen item essential to cut different ingredients. It sure makes cutting of anything easy.

 Apple And Pineapple Corer

A corer is a specialized tool that cuts out the center portion of several fruits like pineapples, apples, guavas, etc. This tool will help you cut out the core easily without cutting any extra flesh off the fruit.

 Vacuum Juice Containers

These prevent the juice from contamination and oxidization. You can keep the juice in these containers for immediate serving.

 Big Juice Cups

It is better to serve with a juice cup because their size is perfect for a juice serving. You can buy them easily from grocery stores or online. Some cups even come with measurements, so you can measure out your juice before drinking.

 Reusable Straws

These straws are a great investment, and they are also great for conserving the ecosystem. Instead of disposable straws, these reusable straws can be easily washed and sterilized whenever needed.

Selecting the Best Juicer

If you are going to live on homemade fresh juices, then investing in a good juicer is better than spending double the money on fixing wrong or low-quality juicers. There are a variety of juicers out there, and you can pick the best by knowing their distinctive features. Here are different juicers you can buy for regular everyday use:

Centrifugal Juicers

With these juicers, ingredients like vegetables and fruits are pushed towards a chute and are passed through into a mesh basket spinning at a high speed. When the ingredients are pushed through this basket with a grated bottom, the juice is separated from the pulp, and the pulp goes into a separate basket.

Masticating Juicers

These juicers are designed with a single gear, and it chews the fruits and vegetables. The fibrous cells are broken down, which releases the juices. The squeezed juices are extracted through a steel screen. These juicers are more efficient than centrifugal juicers because they give a greater quantity of juices and dryer pulp. As they run at low speed, the risk of oxidation and loss of nutrients is quite low.

Twin Gear Juicers

These juicers are slower than the masticating juicers, which means they have a higher yield than masticating juicers. There are two interlocking roller gears in this juicer that slowly squeeze the juice out of the produce.

Norwalk Hydraulic Press

These are the most effective and slowest of all juicers. And if you can buy this expensive juicer, it can be an excellent investment as it will give you the highest yield than all other juicers. This machine then presses the juice out of any product from vegetables to fruits and even wheatgrass.

Chapter 3: The Kitchen Tool Essentials for Smoothies and Juices

Things to Consider Before Buying

If you are planning to buy a juicer and unable to make your mind, then here are some things that you need to think of first:

— First, start by estimating your budget. Some juicers like Norwalk hydraulic press juicer can cost you up to $2500. So even though it is efficient, not everyone can afford it. Think of your budget first, then look for the juicer available in your set range.

— The next important thing is to think about the investment of time. Not everyone can spare time every other day to prepare juices; they need to be stored and prep ahead.

— Cleaning up after juicing produce also takes time. Add the cleanup time to your planning in your schedule. If you can't do this daily, then come with a plan twice or three times per week.

— Then think about the shelf life of the juices you are planning to store. Weigh the pros and cons of juicing daily and storing juices ahead.

— Think about the storage space in your kitchen and then plan to buy the right sized juicer according to this space.

— Finally, think about the ingredients you will be juicing and then buy the juicer best suited for them.

How to Store Your Juices

Smoothies do not have a long shelf life because they usually have a liquid base that can spoil easily if left without proper storage. Among the factors of spoilage, oxidization is another major cause.

1. Always store fresh juices in an airtight container made out of glass. Glass is non-reactive and contains no contaminants, which keeps the juice fresh.

2. Do not leave any space over the juice because empty space means air carrying oxygen which may oxidize the juice. So, fill up your storage container completely with juice.

3. Add a piece of lime, lemon, and grapefruit to the stored juice because a little citrus and Vitamin C will prevent the loss of nutrients.

4. Keep the stored juice in a dark place whenever you are traveling. It is best to keep these juices with ice packs in a cooler bag.

5. At home, you can store the bottled-up juices in the refrigerator for up to 72 hours.

6. After 72 hours of storage, the stored juices lose their nutrients and become more oxidized and darker in color. This oxidation and loss of nutrients also affects the taste of the juice, and they become unpalatable. After this duration, bacteria may also grow in the juice, which might upset your stomach. So, it is best to consume them within 72 hours of storage in the refrigerator.

CHAPTER 04

PLANT-BASED SMOOTHIE & JUICING RECIPES

Breakfast Smoothies

We all need an energizing blend of ingredients to kick start our day, and these breakfast smoothies are a great option to go for. These plant-based breakfast smoothies are prepared using a variety of fiber-packed, protein-rich, nutritious ingredients that can give you a complete serving in a single glass. Fruits loaded with vitamins and antioxidants like blueberries, strawberries, cranberries, blueberries, avocados and peaches, etc., are blended with fresh green veggies, plant-based milk, oats or nuts and seeds in different ways. Adding some superfoods like spirulina powder and vegan protein powder can further increase the nutritional values of these smoothies, making them a perfect fit to pair with every morning meal in a different style.

Chapter 4: Plant-Based Smoothie & Juicing Recipes

Almond Smoothie

Servings: 2

Preparation Time: 10 minutes

Ingredients:

- ¾ cup almonds, chopped
- 2 teaspoons almond butter
- ¼ teaspoon vanilla extract
- 7-8 drops liquid stevia
- 1½ cups unsweetened almond milk
- ¼ cup ice cubes

Instructions:

1. Add all the ingredients in a high-power blender and pulse until creamy and smooth.
2. Pour the smoothie into two glasses and serve immediately.

Nutritional Information per Serving:

Calories	: 336
Fat	: 29.5g
Saturated Fat	: 2.3g
Carbohydrates	: 12.2g
Fiber	: 6.8g
Sugar	: 2.3g
Protein	: 11.7g
Sodium	: 136mg

Banana Oatmeal Smoothie

Servings: 2

Preparation Time: 10 minutes

Ingredients:

- 1½ frozen bananas, peeled and sliced
- ½ cup old-fashioned oats
- 2 tablespoons peanut butter
- 1 tablespoon chia seeds
- 1½ tablespoons maple syrup
- 1½ cups unsweetened almond milk
- ¼ cup ice cubes

Instructions:

1. Add all the ingredients in a high-power blender and pulse until creamy and smooth.
2. Pour the smoothie into two glasses and serve immediately.

Nutritional Information per Serving:

Calories	: 340
Fat	: 13.5g
Saturated Fat	: 2.4g
Carbohydrates	: 52.8g
Fiber	: 7.3g
Sugar	: 2.5g
Protein	: 9.1g
Sodium	: 211mg

Chapter 4: Plant-Based Smoothie & Juicing Recipes

Apple Oatmeal Smoothie

Servings: 2

Preparation Time: 10 minutes

Ingredients:

- 1 medium red delicious apple, peeled and sliced
- 1 small ripe banana, peeled and sliced
- ¼ cup old-fashioned oats
- 1½ cups unsweetened almond milk
- ½ teaspoon ground cinnamon
- 1 cup ice cubes

Instructions:

1. Add all the ingredients in a high-power blender and pulse until creamy and smooth.
2. Pour the smoothie into two glasses and serve immediately.

Nutritional Information per Serving:

Calories	: 179
Fat	: 3.7g
Saturated Fat	: 0.4g
Carbohydrates	: 37.6g
Fiber	: 6.3g
Sugar	: 18.9g
Protein	: 3g
Sodium	: 137mg

Strawberry Oatmeal Smoothie

Servings: 2

Preparation Time: 10 minutes

Ingredients:

- 1½ cups frozen strawberries
- 1 medium banana, peeled and sliced
- ¼ cup old-fashioned oats
- 1 cup coconut yogurt
- ¾ cup unsweetened almond milk

Instructions:

1. Add all the ingredients in a high-power blender and pulse until creamy and smooth.
2. Pour the smoothie into two glasses and serve immediately.

Nutritional Information per Serving:

Calories	: 190
Fat	: 6.5g
Saturated Fat	: 3.8g
Carbohydrates	: 35.3g
Fiber	: 9.1g
Sugar	: 13.6g
Protein	: 3.1g
Sodium	: 165mg

Blackberry & Spinach Smoothie

Servings: 2
Preparation Time: 10 minutes

Ingredients:

- ¾ cup fresh blackberries
- 2 cups fresh spinach leaves
- ¼ cup fresh mint leaves
- 1 tablespoon sunflower seeds
- 1 tablespoon pumpkin seeds
- 1½ cups unsweetened almond milk
- ¼ cup ice cubes

Instructions:

1. Add all the ingredients in a high-power blender and pulse until creamy and smooth.
2. Pour the smoothie into two glasses and serve immediately.

Nutritional Information per Serving:

Calories	: 97
Fat	: 5.g
Saturated Fat	: 0.7g
Carbohydrates	: 9.8g
Fiber	: 5.3g
Sugar	: 2.9g
Protein	: 4.1g
Sodium	: 164mg

Mixed Berries Smoothie

Servings: 2
Preparation Time: 10 minutes

Ingredients:

- 1½ cups frozen mixed berries
- ½ teaspoon vanilla extract
- 1 cup unsweetened coconut milk
- 1 cup fresh orange juice
- ¼ cup ice cubes

Instructions:

1. Add all the ingredients in a high-power blender and pulse until creamy and smooth.
2. Pour the smoothie into two glasses and serve immediately.

Nutritional Information per Serving:

Calories	: 299
Fat	: 17.1g
Saturated Fat	: 15.1g
Carbohydrates	: 28.8g
Fiber	: 4g
Sugar	: 21g
Protein	: 3.1g
Sodium	: 39mg

Chapter 4: Plant-Based Smoothie & Juicing Recipes

Pineapple & Mango Smoothie

Servings: 2

Preparation Time: 10 minutes

Ingredients:

- ½ cup mango, peeled, pitted and chopped
- ½ cup pineapple chunks
- ¼ teaspoon vanilla extract
- ½ cup coconut yogurt
- ¾ cup fresh orange juice
- ¼ cup ice cubes

Instructions:

1. Add all the ingredients in a high-power blender and pulse until creamy and smooth.
2. Pour the smoothie into two glasses and serve immediately.

Nutritional Information per Serving:

Calories	: 114
Fat	: 2.4g
Saturated Fat	: 1.8g
Carbohydrates	: 24.3g
Fiber	: 3.4g
Sugar	: 18.1g
Protein	: 1.2g
Sodium	: 49mg

Kiwi & Banana Smoothie

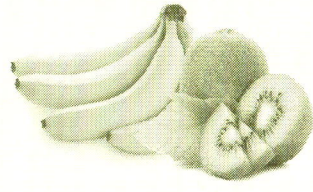

Servings: 2

Preparation Time: 10 minutes

Ingredients:

- 2 frozen bananas, peeled and sliced
- 4 kiwis, peeled and sliced
- 1½ cups unsweetened almond milk
- ½ cup ice cubes

Instructions:

1. Add all the ingredients in a high-power blender and pulse until creamy and smooth.
2. Pour the smoothie into two glasses and serve immediately.

Nutritional Information per Serving:

Calories	: 228
Fat	: 3.8g
Saturated Fat	: 0.4g
Carbohydrates	: 50.7g
Fiber	: 8.4g
Sugar	: 28.1g
Protein	: 3.8g
Sodium	: 141mg

Chapter 4: Plant-Based Smoothie & Juicing Recipes

Orange Smoothie

Servings: 2
Preparation Time: 10 minutes

Ingredients:

- 2 large oranges, peeled, seeded and sectioned
- 2 tablespoons maple syrup
- 1 cup full-fat coconut milk
- ¼ cup ice cubes

Instructions:

1. Add all the ingredients in a high-power blender and pulse until creamy and smooth.
2. Pour the smoothie into two glasses and serve immediately.

Nutritional Information per Serving:

Calories	: 379
Fat	: 24.3g
Saturated Fat	: 22g
Carbohydrates	: 39g
Fiber	: 4.4g
Sugar	: 31.1g
Protein	: 3.7g
Sodium	: 32mg

Green Hemp Smoothie

Servings: 2
Preparation Time: 10 minutes

Ingredients:

- 1 tablespoon raw hemp seeds, shelled
- 2 cups fresh baby spinach
- ½ of avocado, peeled, pitted and chopped
- 4-6 drops liquid stevia
- ¼ teaspoon ground cinnamon
- 2 cups chilled water

Instructions:

1. Add all the ingredients in a high-power blender and pulse until creamy and smooth.
2. Pour the smoothie into two glasses and serve immediately.

Nutritional Information per Serving:

Calories	: 140
Fat	: 12.3g
Saturated Fat	: 2.3g
Carbohydrates	: 6g
Fiber	: 4.5g
Sugar	: 0.4g
Protein	: 3.5g
Sodium	: 27mg

Brain Nourishing Smoothies

The human brain takes a large chunk of energy produced in the body through the consumption of food. Having nutritious, loaded and energizing food on the menu can help boost brain functioning. The brain nourishing smoothies are prepared in such a way that they could provide all the super nutritious and cell-rejuvenating ingredients in a single glass. Nuts like walnuts and almonds are known as great brain boosters, so they are commonly used in these brain-nourishing smoothies. These smoothies are especially healthy for the growing kids, people having loss of concentration and focus, and those suffering from a variety of brain disorders.

Chapter 4: Plant-Based Smoothie & Juicing Recipes

Mocha Chia Smoothie

Servings: 2
Preparation Time: 10 minutes

Ingredients:

- 1 banana, peeled and sliced
- 4 tablespoons rolled oats
- 1 tablespoon chia seeds
- 1 tablespoon cacao powder
- 1 tablespoon maple syrup
- 1 cup cold brewed coffee
- 1 cup unsweetened almond milk

Instructions:

1. Add all the ingredients in a high-power blender and pulse until creamy and smooth.
2. Pour the smoothie into two glasses and serve immediately.

Nutritional Information per Serving:

Calories	: 159
Fat	: 4.4g
Saturated Fat	: 0.7g
Carbohydrates	: 30.9g
Fiber	: 5.1g
Sugar	: 13.3g
Protein	: 3.9g
Sodium	: 94mg

Chocolate Banana Smoothie

Servings: 2
Preparation Time: 10 minutes

Ingredients:

- ½ cups walnuts
- 2 frozen bananas, peeled
- 1 tablespoon coconut butter
- 2 tablespoons cacao powder
- 2 teaspoons lucuma powder
- ½ teaspoon ground cinnamon
- Pinch of salt
- 1½ cups unsweetened almond milk

Instructions:

1. Add all the ingredients in a high-power blender and pulse until creamy and smooth.
2. Pour the smoothie into two glasses and serve immediately.

Nutritional Information per Serving:

Calories	: 399
Fat	: 27g
Saturated Fat	: 6g
Carbohydrates	: 38.3g
Fiber	: 10g
Sugar	: 15.8g
Protein	: 11.1g
Sodium	: 217mg

The Plant-Based Vegan: Juicing and Smoothie Diet Cookbook
200 Delicious Smoothie & Juicing Recipes To Lose Weight, Detox Your Body, and Live A Long Healthy Life

Chapter 4: Plant-Based Smoothie & Juicing Recipes

Blueberry & Avocado Smoothie

Servings: 2

Preparation Time: 10 minutes

Ingredients:

- 2 cups fresh blueberries
- 1 large banana, peeled and sliced
- 1 small avocado, peeled, pitted and chopped
- 1 tablespoon chia seeds
- 1 cup fresh cranberry juice
- ¼ cup ice cubes

Instructions:

1. Add all the ingredients in a high-power blender and pulse until creamy and smooth.
2. Pour the smoothie into two glasses and serve immediately.

Nutritional Information per Serving:

Calories	: 304
Fat	: 12g
Saturated Fat	: 2.5g
Carbohydrates	: 47.9g
Fiber	: 12.3g
Sugar	: 25g
Protein	: 3.7g
Sodium	: 5mg

Berries, Kale & Avocado Smoothie

Servings: 2

Preparation Time: 10 minutes

Ingredients:

- 1 cup frozen blueberries
- 1 cup fresh kale leaves
- ½ of avocado, peeled, pitted and chopped
- 3 Medjool dates, pitted
- ½ teaspoon green spirulina powder
- 2 cups unsweetened soy milk

Instructions:

1. Add all the ingredients in a high-power blender and pulse until creamy and smooth.
2. Pour the smoothie into two glasses and serve immediately.

Nutritional Information per Serving:

Calories	: 389
Fat	: 14.3g
Saturated Fat	: 2.6g
Carbohydrates	: 58.6g
Fiber	: 9.5g
Sugar	: 38.5g
Protein	: 12g
Sodium	: 149mg

The Plant-Based Vegan: Juicing and Smoothie Diet Cookbook
200 Delicious Smoothie & Juicing Recipes To Lose Weight, Detox Your Body, and Live A Long Healthy Life

Limony Blackberry Smoothie

 Servings: 2

Preparation Time: 10 minutes

Ingredients:

- 2 cups frozen blackberries
- 1 small banana, peeled and sliced
- 2 tablespoons fresh lime juice
- 1 tablespoon maple syrup
- 1 teaspoon lime zest, grated
- 1½ cups full-fat coconut milk

Instructions:

1. Add all the ingredients in a high-power blender and pulse until creamy and smooth.
2. Pour the smoothie into two glasses and serve immediately.

Nutritional Information per Serving:

Calories	: 244
Fat	: 8.9g
Saturated Fat	: 8.3g
Carbohydrates	: 42.2g
Fiber	: 4.9g
Sugar	: 29.2g
Protein	: 2.5g
Sodium	: 10mg

Turmeric Fruity Smoothie

 Servings: 2

 Preparation Time: 10 minutes

Ingredients:

- 2 medium frozen bananas, peeled and sliced
- 1 cup frozen mango cubes
- 1 teaspoon fresh turmeric, peeled and grated
- 1 teaspoon fresh ginger, peeled and grated
- 1 tablespoon hemp seeds
- ¼ teaspoon vanilla extract
- 2 cups soy milk

Instructions:

1. Add all the ingredients in a high-power blender and pulse until creamy and smooth.
2. Pour the smoothie into two glasses and serve immediately.

Nutritional Information per Serving:

Calories	: 316
Fat	: 6.9g
Saturated Fat	: 0.9g
Carbohydrates	: 58.4g
Fiber	: 6.3g
Sugar	: 35.6g
Protein	: 11.4g
Sodium	: 128mg

Chapter 4: Plant-Based Smoothie & Juicing Recipes

Kale & Avocado Smoothie

Servings: 2

Preparation Time: 10 minutes

Ingredients:

- 2 cups fresh baby kale
- ½ of avocado, peeled, pitted and chopped
- 1 tablespoon raw hemp seeds, shelled
- 4-6 drops liquid stevia
- ½ teaspoon ground cinnamon
- 2 cups chilled water

Instructions:

1. Add all the ingredients in a high-power blender and pulse until creamy and smooth.
2. Pour the smoothie into two glasses and serve immediately.

Nutritional Information per Serving:

Calories	: 163
Fat	: 11.8g
Saturated Fat	: 2.2g
Carbohydrates	: 11.1g
Fiber	: 5g
Sugar	: 0.6g
Protein	: 5.3g
Sodium	: 32mg

Nutty Spinach Smoothie

Servings: 2

Preparation Time: 10 minutes

Ingredients:

- 2 cups fresh spinach
- 2 tablespoons almonds
- 2 tablespoons walnuts
- 1 tablespoon psyllium seeds
- 1½ cups unsweetened almond milk

Instructions:

1. Add all the ingredients in a high-power blender and pulse until creamy and smooth.
2. Pour the smoothie into two glasses and serve immediately.

Nutritional Information per Serving:

Calories	: 236
Fat	: 11.9g
Saturated Fat	: 1.8g
Carbohydrates	: 10.8g
Fiber	: 6.2g
Sugar	: 3.6g
Protein	: 28g
Sodium	: 217mg

Broccoli, Kale & Apple Smoothie

Servings: 2

Preparation Time: 10 minutes

Ingredients:

- 1 large green apple, peeled, cored and chopped
- ½ cup broccoli florets, chopped
- 2 cups fresh kale leaves
- 1 tablespoon matcha tea powder
- 1½ cups filtered water
- ¼ cup ice cubes

Instructions:

1. Add all the ingredients in a high-power blender and pulse until creamy and smooth.
2. Pour the smoothie into two glasses and serve immediately.

Nutritional Information per Serving:

Calories	: 99
Fat	: 0.3g
Saturated Fat	: 0g
Carbohydrates	: 23.9g
Fiber	: 4.3g
Sugar	: 12g
Protein	: 2.9g
Sodium	: 38mg

Green Pumpkin Seed Smoothie

Servings: 2

Preparation Time: 10 minutes

Ingredients:

- 2 apples, peeled, cored and chopped
- 1 cup frozen blueberries
- 2 cups fresh baby spinach
- ¼ cup pumpkin seeds
- 1½ tablespoons flaxseeds
- 1 tablespoon raw wheat germ
- 4-6 drops liquid stevia

Instructions:

1. Add all the ingredients in a high-power blender and pulse until creamy and smooth.
2. Pour the smoothie into two glasses and serve immediately.

Nutritional Information per Serving:

Calories	: 299
Fat	: 10.7g
Saturated Fat	: 1.8g
Carbohydrates	: 48.7g
Fiber	: 10.4g
Sugar	: 31.1g
Protein	: 8.2g
Sodium	: 31mg

Smoothies to Protect Your Bones & Kidneys

Our bones require lots of calcium for getting the much-needed strength and a good amount of Vitamin C to allow better absorption of calcium in the bones. These smoothies are prepared using ingredients that can provide all the minerals and vitamins that can help improve bone strength. In this section, you will also find smoothies that are good for your kidney. Our kidneys require a constant and controlled supply of sodium and potassium to maintain the internal environment and to remove the unwanted waste and toxins out of the body, and the leafy greens, superfood, nuts, seeds, berries and plant-based ingredients in these smoothies can ensure all of that.

Chapter 4: Plant-Based Smoothie & Juicing Recipes

Blueberry Smoothie

Servings: 2
Preparation Time: 10 minutes

Ingredients:

- 1½ cups frozen blueberries
- ½ cup unsweetened vegan protein powder
- 2 tablespoons maple syrup
- 14 ounces fresh apple juice
- ¼ cup ice cubes

Instructions:

1. Add all the ingredients in a high-power blender and pulse until creamy and smooth.
2. Pour the smoothie into two glasses and serve immediately.

Nutritional Information per Serving:

Calories	: 310
Fat	: 1.5g
Saturated Fat	: 0g
Carbohydrates	: 53g
Fiber	: 2.6g
Sugar	: 22.7g
Protein	: 26.2g
Sodium	: 267mg

Blueberry & Cucumber Smoothie

Servings: 2
Preparation Time: 10 minutes

Ingredients:

- 2 cups fresh blueberries
- 1 large cucumber, peeled and sliced
- 2 tablespoons chia seeds
- Pinch of ground cinnamon
- 2-4 drops liquid stevia
- 1 teaspoon fresh lime juice
- 1 cup coconut water
- 1 cup ice

Instructions:

1. Add all the ingredients in a high-power blender and pulse until creamy and smooth.
2. Pour the smoothie into two glasses and serve immediately.

Nutritional Information per Serving:

Calories	: 189
Fat	: 3.9g
Saturated Fat	: 0.3g
Carbohydrates	: 36.1g
Fiber	: 10.6g
Sugar	: 20g
Protein	: 6g
Sodium	: 130mg

The Plant-Based Vegan: Juicing and Smoothie Diet Cookbook
200 Delicious Smoothie & Juicing Recipes To Lose Weight, Detox Your Body, and Live A Long Healthy Life

Strawberry & Bell Pepper Smoothie

Servings: 2

Preparation Time: 10 minutes

Ingredients:

- 1½ cup frozen strawberries
- 1 frozen banana, peeled
- ½ cup red bell pepper, seeded and cubed
- 1 tablespoon flaxseed
- 1 cup fresh apple juice

Instructions:

1. Add all the ingredients in a high-power blender and pulse until creamy and smooth.
2. Pour the smoothie into two glasses and serve immediately.

Nutritional Information per Serving:

Calories	: 172
Fat	: 1.8g
Saturated Fat	: 0.3g
Carbohydrates	: 39g
Fiber	: 5.3g
Sugar	: 26.1g
Protein	: 2.4g
Sodium	: 8mg

Cranberry Smoothie

Servings: 2

Preparation Time: 10 minutes

Ingredients:

- 1 cup fresh cranberries
- 1½ scoops unsweetened protein powder
- 1 teaspoon vanilla extract
- 3-4 drops liquid stevia
- 1¼ cups unsweetened almond milk
- ½ cup ice cubes

Instructions:

1. Add all the ingredients in a high-power blender and pulse until creamy and smooth.
2. Pour the smoothie into two glasses and serve immediately.

Nutritional Information per Serving:

Calories	: 148
Fat	: 3g
Saturated Fat	: 0.2g
Carbohydrates	: 6.5g
Fiber	: 2.6g
Sugar	: 2.3g
Protein	: 19.6g
Sodium	: 311mg

Chapter 4: Plant-Based Smoothie & Juicing Recipes

Raspberry & Peach Smoothie

 Servings: 2

Preparation Time: 10 minutes

Ingredients:

- 1 cup frozen raspberries
- 2 medium peaches, pitted and sliced
- ½ cup silken tofu
- 1 tablespoon maple syrup
- 1½ cups unsweetened almond milk
- ¼ cup ice cubes

Instructions:

1. Add all the ingredients in a high-power blender and pulse until creamy and smooth.
2. Pour the smoothie into two glasses and serve immediately.

Nutritional Information per Serving:

Calories	: 191
Fat	: 6.1g
Saturated Fat	: 0.8g
Carbohydrates	: 30.6g
Fiber	: 7.6g
Sugar	: 23.1g
Protein	: 8.1g
Sodium	: 144mg

Pineapple Smoothie

 Servings: 2

 Preparation Time: 10 minutes

Ingredients:

- 2 cups pineapple chunks
- 2 scoops unsweetened vegan protein powder
- 1½ cups water
- ¼ cup ice cubes

Instructions:

1. Add all the ingredients in a high-power blender and pulse until creamy and smooth.
2. Pour the smoothie into two glasses and serve immediately.

Nutritional Information per Serving:

Calories	: 198
Fat	: 1.3g
Saturated Fat	: 0g
Carbohydrates	: 21.7g
Fiber	: 2.3g
Sugar	: 16.3g
Protein	: 26.2g
Sodium	: 266mg

Chapter 4: Plant-Based Smoothie & Juicing Recipes

Cherry & Blueberry Smoothie

Servings: 2

Preparation Time: 10 minutes

Ingredients:

- 1¼ cups frozen blueberries
- 1 cup frozen unsweetened cherries
- 1 small banana, peeled and sliced
- 1¾ cups unsweetened almond milk

Instructions:

1. Add all the ingredients in a high-power blender and pulse until creamy and smooth.
2. Pour the smoothie into two glasses and serve immediately.

Nutritional Information per Serving:

Calories	: 203
Fat	: 2.3g
Saturated Fat	: 0.2g
Carbohydrates	: 43g
Fiber	: 5.5g
Sugar	: 24.7g
Protein	: 6.5g
Sodium	: 156mg

Peach Smoothie

Servings: 2

Preparation Time: 10 minutes

Ingredients:

- 1½ cups fresh peaches, pitted
- 1 scoop unflavored vegan protein powder
- 1 tablespoon maple syrup
- 2 cups chilled unsweetened almond milk

Instructions:

1. Add all the ingredients in a high-power blender and pulse until creamy and smooth.
2. Pour the smoothie into two glasses and serve immediately.

Nutritional Information per Serving:

Calories	: 165
Fat	: 4.6g
Saturated Fat	: 0.3g
Carbohydrates	: 19.2g
Fiber	: 2.7g
Sugar	: 16.5g
Protein	: 14.6g
Sodium	: 321mg

Chapter 4: Plant-Based Smoothie & Juicing Recipes

Kale & Pineapple Smoothie

Servings: 2

Preparation Time: 10 minutes

Ingredients:

- 1½ cups fresh kale, trimmed and chopped
- 1 frozen banana, peeled and chopped
- ½ cup fresh pineapple chunks
- 1 cup unsweetened coconut milk
- ½ cup fresh orange juice
- ½ cup ice

Instructions:

1. Add all the ingredients in a high-power blender and pulse until creamy and smooth.
2. Pour the smoothie into two glasses and serve immediately.

Nutritional Information per Serving:

Calories	: 148
Fat	: 2.4g
Saturated Fat	: 2.1g
Carbohydrates	: 31.6g
Fiber	: 3.5g
Sugar	: 16.5g
Protein	: 2.8g
Sodium	: 23mg

Cabbage & Cucumber Smoothie

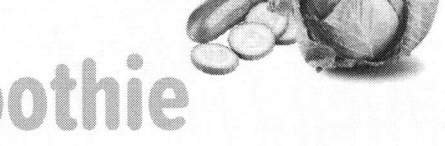

Servings: 2

Preparation Time: 10 minutes

Ingredients:

- 1 cup green cabbage, shredded or chopped
- 1 cucumber, peeled and chopped
- 1 frozen banana, peeled
- 2 scoops unsweetened vegan protein powder
- 1½ cups unsweetened coconut milk

Instructions:

1. Add all the ingredients in a high-power blender and pulse until creamy and smooth.
2. Pour the smoothie into two glasses and serve immediately.

Nutritional Information per Serving:

Calories	: 470
Fat	: 26.2g
Saturated Fat	: 22.6g
Carbohydrates	: 25.5g
Fiber	: 3.2g
Sugar	: 15.4g
Protein	: 29.7g
Sodium	: 330mg

Anti-Aging Smoothies

Aging is a slow process, but it speeds up with a poor diet and lifestyle. By eating healthy and living an active life, we can slow down this process. In this section, there are smoothies that can help you fight the signs of aging. Here ingredients like vegan protein powders, berries, nuts, seeds, plant-based milk, lots of fruits, and mixed greens can help elevate the body's metabolic rates and increase cell activity. These ingredients help reproduce new and healthy cells while removing the old cells from the body. Moreover, these smoothies are free from food items like processed sugar and canned food that speeds up aging. Adding these smoothies to your routine menu can make you active and younger-looking.

Chapter 4: Plant-Based Smoothie & Juicing Recipes

Chocolate Date Smoothie

Servings: 2
Preparation Time: 10 minutes

Ingredients:

- 6-8 dates, pitted
- ¾ cup walnuts
- 2 tablespoons cacao powder
- ¼ teaspoon vanilla extract
- Pinch of ground cinnamon
- 1½ cups unsweetened almond milk
- ¼ cup ice cubes

Instructions:

1. Add all the ingredients in a high-power blender and pulse until creamy and smooth.
2. Pour the smoothie into two glasses and serve immediately.

Nutritional Information per Serving:

Calories	: 183
Fat	: 10.6g
Saturated Fat	: 1.5g
Carbohydrates	: 24.3g
Fiber	: 5g
Sugar	: 16.1g
Protein	: 4g
Sodium	: 136mg

Banana & Blackberries Smoothie

Servings: 2
Preparation Time: 10 minutes

Ingredients:

- 1 cup fresh blackberries
- 2 medium bananas, peeled and sliced
- 2 teaspoons ground chia seeds
- 1 scoop unsweetened vegan protein powder
- 1½ cups chilled unsweetened almond milk

Instructions:

1. Add all the ingredients in a high-power blender and pulse until creamy and smooth.
2. Pour the smoothie into two glasses and serve immediately.

Nutritional Information per Serving:

Calories	: 239
Fat	: 5.1g
Saturated Fat	: 0.5g
Carbohydrates	: 37g
Fiber	: 9g
Sugar	: 17.9g
Protein	: 16.5g
Sodium	: 270mg

Chapter 4: Plant-Based Smoothie & Juicing Recipes

Pear & Cherry Smoothie

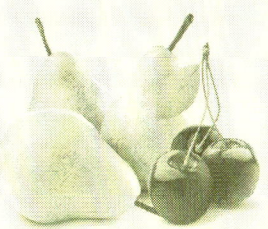

🍽 **Servings:** 2

🕐 **Preparation Time:** 10 minutes

Ingredients:

- 1 large pear, peeled, cored and chopped
- 2 cups frozen cherries, pitted
- 2 Medjool dates, pitted and chopped
- 2 tablespoons sunflower seeds
- 1 teaspoon maca powder
- 1½ cups chilled unsweetened almond milk

Instructions:

1. Add all the ingredients in a high-power blender and pulse until creamy and smooth.
2. Pour the smoothie into two glasses and serve immediately.

Nutritional Information per Serving:

Calories	: 242
Fat	: 4.9g
Saturated Fat	: 0.5g
Carbohydrates	: 51.2g
Fiber	: 7.8g
Sugar	: 39g
Protein	: 4.2g
Sodium	: 138mg

Strawberry & Pistachio Smoothie

🍽 **Servings:** 2

🕐 **Preparation Time:** 10 minutes

Ingredients:

- 2 cups fresh strawberries, hulled and sliced
- 1 medium banana, peeled and sliced
- ¼ cup raw pistachios
- 2 tablespoons ground chia seeds
- ½ cup plain coconut yogurt
- 1 cup coconut water
- ¼ cup ice cubes

Instructions:

1. Add all the ingredients in a high-power blender and pulse until creamy and smooth.
2. Pour the smoothie into two glasses and serve immediately.

Nutritional Information per Serving:

Calories	: 202
Fat	: 7.6g
Saturated Fat	: 2.6g
Carbohydrates	: 35.6g
Fiber	: 9.9g
Sugar	: 18.4g
Protein	: 4.8g
Sodium	: 216mg

The Plant-Based Vegan: Juicing and Smoothie Diet Cookbook
200 Delicious Smoothie & Juicing Recipes To Lose Weight, Detox Your Body, and Live A Long Healthy Life

Raspberry & Kale Smoothie

 Servings: 2

 Preparation Time: 10 minutes

Ingredients:

- 1 cup fresh raspberries
- 1 small frozen banana, peeled and sliced
- 2 cups fresh baby kale, chopped
- 2 Medjool dates, pitted and chopped
- 1½ cups unsweetened almond milk
- ¼ cup ice cubes

Instructions:

1. Add all the ingredients in a high-power blender and pulse until creamy and smooth.
2. Pour the smoothie into two glasses and serve immediately.

Nutritional Information per Serving:

Calories	: 220
Fat	: 3.2g
Saturated Fat	: 0.3g
Carbohydrates	: 48.4g
Fiber	: 9.1g
Sugar	: 26.9g
Protein	: 5g
Sodium	: 165mg

Raspberry & Blackberry Smoothie

 Servings: 2

Preparation Time: 10 minutes

Ingredients:

- 1½ cups frozen raspberries
- 1 cup frozen blackberries
- 2 tablespoons ground flaxseeds
- 1 tablespoon goji berry powder
- 1 tablespoon maple syrup
- 1½ cups unsweetened almond milk
- ¼ cup ice cubes

Instructions:

1. Add all the ingredients in a high-power blender and pulse until creamy and smooth.
2. Pour the smoothie into two glasses and serve immediately.

Nutritional Information per Serving:

Calories	: 187
Fat	: 5.8g
Saturated Fat	: 0.6g
Carbohydrates	: 30.6g
Fiber	: 12.5g
Sugar	: 15.1g
Protein	: 4.7g
Sodium	: 155mg

Chapter 4: Plant-Based Smoothie & Juicing Recipes

Blackberry & Strawberry Smoothie

Servings: 2

Preparation Time: 10 minutes

Ingredients:

- 1 cup frozen blackberries
- 1 cup frozen strawberries
- 1 small banana, peeled and sliced
- 2 tablespoons hemp seeds
- ½ cup plain coconut yogurt
- 1¼ cups fresh orange juice

Instructions:

1. Add all the ingredients in a high-power blender and pulse until creamy and smooth.
2. Pour the smoothie into two glasses and serve immediately.

Nutritional Information per Serving:

Calories	: 244
Fat	: 6.5g
Saturated Fat	: 2.1g
Carbohydrates	: 45.6g
Fiber	: 9.4g
Sugar	: 27.8g
Protein	: 5.7g
Sodium	: 51mg

Watermelon & Apple Smoothie

Servings: 2

Preparation Time: 10 minutes

Ingredients:

- 2 cups frozen watermelon, peeled, seeded and chopped
- 1 large apple, peeled, cored and chopped
- 1 frozen banana, peeled and sliced
- 1 tablespoon chia seeds
- 1½ cups unsweetened almond milk

Instructions:

1. Add all the ingredients in a high-power blender and pulse until creamy and smooth.
2. Pour the smoothie into two glasses and serve immediately.

Nutritional Information per Serving:

Calories	: 201
Fat	: 4.5g
Saturated Fat	: 0.5g
Carbohydrates	: 43.3g
Fiber	: 6.8g
Sugar	: 28.2g
Protein	: 3.3g
Sodium	: 139mg

Chapter 4: Plant-Based Smoothie & Juicing Recipes

Papaya Smoothie

Servings: 2

Preparation Time: 10 minutes

Ingredients:

- 2 cups papaya, peeled and sliced
- 1 large banana, peeled and sliced
- 1½ cups unsweetened almond milk
- ½ cup ice cubes

Instructions:

1. Add all the ingredients in a high-power blender and pulse until creamy and smooth.
2. Pour the smoothie into two glasses and serve immediately.

Nutritional Information per Serving:

Calories	: 145
Fat	: 3.2g
Saturated Fat	: 0.4g
Carbohydrates	: 30.7g
Fiber	: 4.8g
Sugar	: 18.5g
Protein	: 2.1g
Sodium	: 148mg

Lettuce & Banana Smoothie

Servings: 2

Preparation Time: 10 minutes

Ingredients:

- 2 medium frozen bananas, peeled and sliced
- ½ cup avocado, peeled, pitted and chopped
- 2 cups fresh lettuce leaves, chopped
- ¼ cup fresh mint leaves
- 2 teaspoons flaxseed meal
- 1 teaspoon maple syrup
- 1½ cups unsweetened coconut milk

Instructions:

1. Add all the ingredients in a high-power blender and pulse until creamy and smooth.
2. Pour the smoothie into two glasses and serve immediately.

Nutritional Information per Serving:

Calories	: 187
Fat	: 5.8g
Saturated Fat	: 0.6g
Carbohydrates	: 30.6g
Fiber	: 12.5g
Sugar	: 15.1g
Protein	: 4.7g
Sodium	: 155mg

Antioxidant Smoothies

Antioxidants are the free radical scavengers, meaning that they actively hunt the cell-damaging free radicals in the body and remove them from the body. Ingredients like spinach, spirulina, kale, celery, avocado, nuts, and seeds are loaded with antioxidants. The following smoothies are created using different combinations of these antioxidants rich ingredients. By increasing the intake of these smoothies, a person can easily reduce the overall oxidative stress of the body. Evidence suggests that free radicals in the body and the increase of oxidative stress are linked to cancer, heart diseases, arthritis, immune deficiency, and respiratory diseases. Having these smoothies will counter your oxidative stress and decrease the risk of the diseases mentioned above.

Spirulina Blueberry Smoothie

Servings: 2

Preparation Time: 10 minutes

Ingredients:

- 2 cups fresh blueberries
- 2 teaspoons blue spirulina powder
- 3-4 drops liquid stevia
- 1½ cups unsweetened almond milk
- ½ cup ice cubes

Instructions:

1. Add all the ingredients in a high-power blender and pulse until creamy and smooth.
2. Pour the smoothie into two glasses and serve immediately.

Nutritional Information per Serving:

Calories	: 120
Fat	: 3.3g
Saturated Fat	: 0.3g
Carbohydrates	: 23.1g
Fiber	: 4.3g
Sugar	: 14.5g
Protein	: 3.2g
Sodium	: 160mg

Berries & Beet Smoothie

Servings: 2

Preparation Time: 10 minutes

Ingredients:

- 1 cup fresh raspberries
- 1 cup fresh strawberries
- 1 beet, trimmed, peeled and chopped
- ¼ cup rolled oats
- 2 teaspoons maca powder
- 1 teaspoon coconut oil
- 1½ cups unsweetened almond milk
- ¼ cup ice cubes

Instructions:

1. Add all the ingredients in a high-power blender and pulse until creamy and smooth.
2. Pour the smoothie into two glasses and serve immediately.

Nutritional Information per Serving:

Calories	: 172
Fat	: 6.3g
Saturated Fat	: 2.3g
Carbohydrates	: 27.3g
Fiber	: 8.6g
Sugar	: 10.7g
Protein	: 4.5g
Sodium	: 175mg

Chapter 4: Plant-Based Smoothie & Juicing Recipes

Fruity Beet Smoothie

Servings: 2

Preparation Time: 10 minutes

Ingredients:

- 1 cup frozen blueberries
- 1 cup frozen pineapple
- 1 medium beet, trimmed, peeled and chopped
- 1 tablespoon chia seeds
- 1-2 teaspoons agave nectar
- ½ cup plain coconut yogurt
- 1½ cup unsweetened almond milk

Instructions:

1. Add all the ingredients in a high-power blender and pulse until creamy and smooth.
2. Pour the smoothie into two glasses and serve immediately.

Nutritional Information per Serving:

Calories	: 184
Fat	: 6.3g
Saturated Fat	: 2.1g
Carbohydrates	: 35g
Fiber	: 8.1g
Sugar	: 22.3g
Protein	: 3.3g
Sodium	: 223mg

Raspberry & Pomegranate Smoothie

Servings: 2

Preparation Time: 10 minutes

Ingredients:

- 2 cups frozen raspberries
- 1 large banana, peeled and sliced
- 2 tablespoons hemp seeds
- 1½ cups fresh pomegranate juice

Instructions:

1. Add all the ingredients in a high-power blender and pulse until creamy and smooth.
2. Pour the smoothie into two glasses and serve immediately.

Nutritional Information per Serving:

Calories	: 297
Fat	: 4.5g
Saturated Fat	: 0.3g
Carbohydrates	: 58.5g
Fiber	: 10g
Sugar	: 39.3g
Protein	: 5.5g
Sodium	: 13mg

The Plant-Based Vegan: Juicing and Smoothie Diet Cookbook
200 Delicious Smoothie & Juicing Recipes To Lose Weight, Detox Your Body, and Live A Long Healthy Life

Chapter 4: Plant-Based Smoothie & Juicing Recipes

Pomegranate, Cherries & Cabbage Smoothie

🛎 **Servings:** 2

🕒 **Preparation Time:** 10 minutes

Ingredients:

- 2 cups fresh red cabbage, chopped
- 1 cup pomegranate seeds
- 1 cup frozen cherries
- ¼ cup goji berries, soaked in water
- 1-2 tablespoons maple syrup
- 1 cup chilled water

Instructions:

1. Add all the ingredients in a high-power blender and pulse until creamy and smooth.
2. Strain the smoothie into two glasses and serve immediately.

Nutritional Information per Serving:

Calories	: 184
Fat	: 6.3g
Saturated Fat	: 2.1g
Carbohydrates	: 35g
Fiber	: 8.1g
Sugar	: 22.3g
Protein	: 3.3g
Sodium	: 223mg

Blueberry & Pomegranate Smoothie

🛎 **Servings:** 2

🕒 **Preparation Time:** 10 minutes

Ingredients:

- 2 cups frozen blueberries
- 2-3 drops liquid stevia
- ½ cup fresh pomegranate juice
- 1 cup unsweetened almond milk

Instructions:

1. Add all the ingredients in a high-power blender and pulse until creamy and smooth.
2. Pour the smoothie into two glasses and serve immediately.

Nutritional Information per Serving:

Calories	: 141
Fat	: 2.3g
Saturated Fat	: 0.2g
Carbohydrates	: 31.3g
Fiber	: 4g
Sugar	: 22.9g
Protein	: 1.9g
Sodium	: 95mg

Chocolate Raspberry Smoothie

Servings: 2

Preparation Time: 10 minutes

Ingredients:

- 2 cups fresh raspberries
- 1 banana, peeled and sliced
- ½ cup vegan dark chocolate chips
- 1½ cups unsweetened almond milk
- ¼ cup ice cubes

Instructions:

1. Add all the ingredients in a high-power blender and pulse until creamy and smooth.
2. Pour the smoothie into two glasses and serve immediately.

Nutritional Information per Serving:

Calories	: 286
Fat	: 11.6g
Saturated Fat	: 5.3g
Carbohydrates	: 49.7g
Fiber	: 10.3g
Sugar	: 28.7g
Protein	: 4.9g
Sodium	: 137mg

Strawberry, Celery & Greens Smoothie

Servings: 2

Preparation Time: 10 minutes

Ingredients:

- 1½ cups frozen strawberries
- 2 cups fresh mixed greens
- 1 cup celery stalk, chopped
- 1 (2-inch) piece fresh ginger, peeled and chopped
- 1 scoop hemp protein powder
- 1½ cup filtered water

Instructions:

1. Add all the ingredients in a high-power blender and pulse until creamy and smooth.
2. Pour the smoothie into two glasses and serve immediately.

Nutritional Information per Serving:

Calories	: 130
Fat	: 3.6g
Saturated Fat	: 0.4g
Carbohydrates	: 16.8g
Fiber	: 6.8g
Sugar	: 7g
Protein	: 9.4g
Sodium	: 71mg

Kale & Cucumber Smoothie

 Servings: 2

 Preparation Time: 10 minutes

Ingredients:

- 2 teaspoons green spirulina powder
- 1½ cups fresh kale
- 1 cup cucumber, peeled and chopped
- 1 tablespoon chia seeds
- 1½ cups unsweetened almond milk
- ¼ cup ice cubes

Instructions:

1. Add all the ingredients in a high-power blender and pulse until creamy and smooth.
2. Pour the smoothie into two glasses and serve immediately.

Nutritional Information per Serving:

Calories	: 84
Fat	: 4.1g
Saturated Fat	: 0.4g
Carbohydrates	: 10.7g
Fiber	: 3.1g
Sugar	: 0.9g
Protein	: 4.7g
Sodium	: 182mg

Kale & Celery Smoothie

 Servings: 2

 Preparation Time: 10 minutes

Ingredients:

- 2 cups fresh kale
- 1 celery stalk
- ½ of avocado, peeled, pitted and chopped
- 1 teaspoon fresh ginger, peeled and chopped
- 1½ cups unsweetened almond milk
- ¼ cup ice cubes

Instructions:

1. Add all the ingredients in a high-power blender and pulse until creamy and smooth.
2. Pour the smoothie into two glasses and serve immediately.

Nutritional Information per Serving:

Calories	: 170
Fat	: 12.5g
Saturated Fat	: 2.3g
Carbohydrates	: 13.7g
Fiber	: 5.4g
Sugar	: 0.4g
Protein	: 3.8g
Sodium	: 174mg

Cleansing Smoothies

Because of all the metabolic processes in the body, our blood receives large amounts of harmful radicals, toxins and waste products. The longer these elements are in the body, the greater the damage they cause. By consuming the cleansing smoothies, you can speed up the detoxification process. These smoothies are prepared using ingredients rich in antioxidants and anti-inflammatory elements. Fruits and vegetables rich in fibers and phytonutrients along with nuts, seeds and some super-foods are used in various combinations to prepare these cleansing smoothies. Having a glass of these cleansing smoothies in the morning or at the end of the day, will help reduce the toxins in your body.

Spiced Smoothie

Servings: 2
Preparation Time: 10 minutes

Ingredients:

- 2 tablespoons chia seeds
- 1 tablespoon ground turmeric
- 1 teaspoon ground cinnamon
- 1 teaspoon ground ginger
- ¼ teaspoon ground cardamom
- Pinch of ground black pepper
- 2 tablespoons MCT oil
- 2 teaspoons stevia powder
- 1¾ cups unsweetened almond milk
- ¼ cup ice cubes

Instructions:

1. Add all the ingredients in a high-power blender and pulse until creamy and smooth.
2. Pour the smoothie into two glasses and serve immediately.

Nutritional Information per Serving:

Calories	: 183
Fat	: 20.4g
Saturated Fat	: 14.6g
Carbohydrates	: 8.7g
Fiber	: 4.9g
Sugar	: 0.2g
Protein	: 2.8g
Sodium	: 159mg

Pineapple & Turmeric Smoothie

 Servings: 2
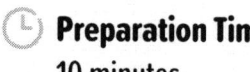 **Preparation Time:** 10 minutes

Ingredients:

- 1½ cups pineapple, chopped
- 1 (1-inch) piece fresh ginger, peeled and chopped
- 1 teaspoon ground turmeric
- 1 teaspoon natural immune support
- 1 teaspoon chia seeds
- 1 cup cold green tea
- ½ cup ice cubes

Instructions:

1. Add all the ingredients in a high-power blender and pulse until creamy and smooth.
2. Pour the smoothie into two glasses and serve immediately.

Nutritional Information per Serving:

Calories	: 104
Fat	: 1.1g
Saturated Fat	: 0.1g
Carbohydrates	: 24.9g
Fiber	: 2.9g
Sugar	: 18.8g
Protein	: 1.3g
Sodium	: 12mg

Chapter 4: Plant-Based Smoothie & Juicing Recipes

Pineapple & Cucumber Smoothie

Servings: 2

Preparation Time: 10 minutes

Ingredients:

- 1 cup pineapple, chopped
- 1 cucumber, peeled and chopped
- 4 Medjool dates, pitted
- 2 tablespoons fresh lemon juice
- 1½ cups filtered water

Instructions:

1. Add all the ingredients in a high-power blender and pulse until creamy and smooth.
2. Pour the smoothie into two glasses and serve immediately.

Nutritional Information per Serving:

Calories	: 193
Fat	: 0.4g
Saturated Fat	: 0.2g
Carbohydrates	: 49.6g
Fiber	: 5.1g
Sugar	: 39.2g
Protein	: 3.1g
Sodium	: 7mg

Cranberry & Grapefruit Smoothie

Servings: 2

Preparation Time: 10 minutes

Ingredients:

- ½ cup fresh cranberries
- 2 grapefruit, peeled, seeded and sectioned
- 1 frozen banana, peeled and sliced
- 1 tablespoon agave nectar
- ¾ cup fresh orange juice
- ½ cup unsweetened almond milk
- ¼ cup ice cubes

Instructions:

1. Add all the ingredients in a high-power blender and pulse until creamy and smooth.
2. Pour the smoothie into two glasses and serve immediately.

Nutritional Information per Serving:

Calories	: 190
Fat	: 1.4g
Saturated Fat	: 0.2g
Carbohydrates	: 44.5g
Fiber	: 4.9g
Sugar	: 2.3g
Protein	: 2.3g
Sodium	: 46mg

Chapter 4: Plant-Based Smoothie & Juicing Recipes

Watermelon & Strawberry Smoothie

Servings: 2

Preparation Time: 10 minutes

Ingredients:

- 1½ cups fresh watermelon, seeded and cubed
- 1 cup frozen strawberries
- ½ of frozen banana, peeled and sliced
- 1 tablespoon hemp seeds
- 2 tablespoons fresh lime juice
- 1 cup unsweetened almond milk

Instructions:

1. Add all the ingredients in a high-power blender and pulse until creamy and smooth.
2. Pour the smoothie into two glasses and serve immediately.

Nutritional Information per Serving:

Calories	: 126
Fat	: 3.9g
Saturated Fat	: 0.4g
Carbohydrates	: 222.2g
Fiber	: 3g
Sugar	: 14.1g
Protein	: 3.2g
Sodium	: 93mg

Pineapple & Grapefruit Smoothie

Servings: 2

Preparation Time: 10 minutes

Ingredients:

- 3 grapefruit, peeled, seeded and chopped
- ½ cup frozen pineapple chunks
- 1½ cups unsweetened almond milk
- ¼ cup ice cubes

Instructions:

1. Add all the ingredients in a high-power blender and pulse until creamy and smooth.
2. Pour the smoothie into two glasses and serve immediately.

Nutritional Information per Serving:

Calories	: 112
Fat	: 2.9g
Saturated Fat	: 0.3g
Carbohydrates	: 22.4g
Fiber	: 3.4g
Sugar	: 17.5g
Protein	: 2.2g
Sodium	: 126mg

Berries & Pomegranate Smoothie

Servings: 2
Preparation Time: 10 minutes

Ingredients:

- 1½ cups fresh mixed berries
- 1 frozen l banana, peeled and sliced
- 1 cup fresh pomegranate juice
- ½ cup chilled water

Instructions:

1. Add all the ingredients in a high-power blender and pulse until creamy and smooth.
2. Pour the smoothie into two glasses and serve immediately.

Nutritional Information per Serving:

Calories	: 188
Fat	: 0.6g
Saturated Fat	: 0.1g
Carbohydrates	: 44.7g
Fiber	: 5.3g
Sugar	: 31.7g
Protein	: 1.9g
Sodium	: 8mg

Herbed Greens Smoothie

Servings: 2
Preparation Time: 10 minutes

Ingredients:

- 1 cup fresh spinach
- ¼ cup fresh kale
- ¼ cup fresh Swiss chard
- ¼ cup fresh mustard greens
- ¼ cup fresh parsley
- ¼ cup fresh cilantro
- ¼ cup fresh basil leaves
- 1 large apple, peeled, cored and sliced
- 2 tablespoon fresh lime juice
- 2 tablespoons maple syrup
- 2 cups chilled water

Instructions:

1. Add all the ingredients in a high-power blender and pulse until creamy and smooth.
2. Pour the smoothie into two glasses and serve immediately.

Nutritional Information per Serving:

Calories	: 125
Fat	: 0.4g
Saturated Fat	: 0g
Carbohydrates	: 31.5g
Fiber	: 3.8g
Sugar	: 23.8g
Protein	: 1.6g
Sodium	: 35mg

Minty Green Smoothie

Servings: 2

Preparation Time: 10 minutes

Ingredients:

- 1 cup fresh kale leaves
- 1 small cucumber, peeled and chopped
- ½ of avocado, peeled, pitted and chopped
- ¼ cup fresh mint leaves
- 1 tablespoon almond butter
- 1 tablespoon fresh lemon juice
- 1¼ cups unsweetened almond milk
- ½ cup ice cubes

Instructions:

1. Add all the ingredients in a high-power blender and pulse until creamy and smooth.
2. Pour the smoothie into two glasses and serve immediately.

Nutritional Information per Serving:

Calories	: 195
Fat	: 15.2g
Saturated Fat	: 2.4g
Carbohydrates	: 13.8g
Fiber	: 6g
Sugar	: 2g
Protein	: 5.1g
Sodium	: 137mg

Spinach & Banana Smoothie

 Servings: 2

 Preparation Time: 10 minutes

Ingredients:

- 2 bananas, peeled and sliced
- 2 cups fresh baby spinach
- 2 tablespoons almond butter
- 1½ cups unsweetened almond milk
- ¼ cup ice cubes

Instructions:

1. Add all the ingredients in a high-power blender and pulse until creamy and smooth.
2. Pour the smoothie into two glasses and serve immediately.

Nutritional Information per Serving:

Calories	: 240
Fat	: 12.1g
Saturated Fat	: 1.1g
Carbohydrates	: 32.5g
Fiber	: 6.1g
Sugar	: 15.3g
Protein	: 6.3g
Sodium	: 161mg

Diabetic Smoothies

People already suffering from diabetes or having pre-diabetes can both consume these smoothies to increase their caloric intake without increasing the sugar and carb intake. Diabetic individuals suffer from low insulin production or insulin resistance; in both cases, the blood glucose levels can only be controlled by consuming only low-glycemic food. High glycemic food is not suitable for diabetic patients, and therefore these smoothies are only created with a blend of low-carb and low-glycemic food. In this way, the blood glucose levels remained maintained.

Chapter 4: Plant-Based Smoothie & Juicing Recipes

Strawberry & Spinach Smoothie

Servings: 2

Preparation Time: 10 minutes

Ingredients:

- 2 cups fresh spinach
- ¾ cup frozen strawberries, sliced
- 1½ cups unsweetened almond milk

Instructions:

1. Add all the ingredients in a high-power blender and pulse until creamy and smooth.
2. Pour the smoothie into two glasses and serve immediately.

Nutritional Information per Serving:

Calories	: 54
Fat	: 2.9g
Saturated Fat	: 0.3g
Carbohydrates	: 6.7g
Fiber	: 2.5g
Sugar	: 2.8g
Protein	: 2g
Sodium	: 159mg

Avocado & Mint Smoothie

Servings: 2

Preparation Time: 10 minutes

Ingredients:

- 1 avocado, peeled, pitted and chopped
- 12-14 fresh large mint leaves
- 2 tablespoons fresh lime juice
- ½ teaspoon vanilla extract
- 1½ cups unsweetened almond milk
- ¼ cup ice, crushed

Instructions:

1. Add all the ingredients in a high-power blender and pulse until creamy and smooth.
2. Pour the smoothie into two glasses and serve immediately.

Nutritional Information per Serving:

Calories	: 214
Fat	: 18.5g
Saturated Fat	: 2.6g
Carbohydrates	: 11.7g
Fiber	: 8.9g
Sugar	: 0.4g
Protein	: 3.3g
Sodium	: 45mg

Chapter 4: Plant-Based Smoothie & Juicing Recipes

Spinach & Avocado Smoothie

 Servings: 2

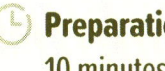 **Preparation Time:** 10 minutes

Ingredients:

- ½ of large avocado, peeled, pitted and chopped roughly
- 2 cups fresh spinach
- 1½ cups unsweetened almond milk

Instructions:

1. Add all the ingredients in a high-power blender and pulse until creamy and smooth.
2. Pour the smoothie into two glasses and serve immediately.

Nutritional Information per Serving:

Calories	: 153
Fat	: 13.8g
Saturated Fat	: 2.6g
Carbohydrates	: 7.5g
Fiber	: 5.2g
Sugar	: 0.4g
Protein	: 2.7g
Sodium	: 162mg

Matcha Chia Seed Smoothie

 Servings: 2

 Preparation Time: 10 minutes

Ingredients:

- 2 tablespoons chia seeds
- 2 teaspoons matcha green tea powder
- ½ teaspoon fresh lime juice
- ¼ cup coconut yogurt
- 1¼ cups unsweetened coconut milk
- ¼ cup ice cubes

Instructions:

1. Add all the ingredients in a high-power blender and pulse until creamy and smooth.
2. Pour the smoothie into two glasses and serve immediately.

Nutritional Information per Serving:

Calories	: 276
Fat	: 24.5g
Saturated Fat	: 20.2g
Carbohydrates	: 8.2g
Fiber	: 2.5g
Sugar	: 4.8g
Protein	: 4.9g
Sodium	: 54mg

Greens & Cucumber Smoothie

Servings: 2
Preparation Time: 10 minutes

Ingredients:

- 1 large cucumber, peeled and chopped
- 2 cups fresh baby greens
- ¼ cup fresh mint leaves
- 2 tablespoons fresh lime juice
- 2 cups chilled unsweetened almond milk

Instructions:

1. Add all the ingredients in a high-power blender and pulse until creamy and smooth.
2. Pour the smoothie into two glasses and serve immediately.

Nutritional Information per Serving:

Calories	: 72
Fat	: 3.8g
Saturated Fat	: 0.4g
Carbohydrates	: 9.2g
Fiber	: 2.9g
Sugar	: 2.9g
Protein	: 2.7g
Sodium	: 190mg

Zucchini & Spinach Smoothie

Servings: 2
Preparation Time: 10 minutes

Ingredients:

- 1 small zucchini, peeled and sliced
- ¾ cup fresh spinach, chopped
- 1 teaspoon ground cinnamon
- 1½ cups unsweetened almond milk
- ½ cup ice cubes

Instructions:

1. Add all the ingredients in a high-power blender and pulse until creamy and smooth.
2. Pour the smoothie into two glasses and serve immediately.

Nutritional Information per Serving:

Calories	: 45
Fat	: 2.8g
Saturated Fat	: 0.3g
Carbohydrates	: 4.8g
Fiber	: 2.3g
Sugar	: 1.1g
Protein	: 1.8g
Sodium	: 150mg

Cucumber & Parsley Smoothie

 Servings: 2

Preparation Time: 10 minutes

Ingredients:

- 2 cups cucumber, peeled and chopped
- 2 cups fresh parsley
- 1 (1-inch) piece fresh ginger root, peeled and chopped
- 2 tablespoons fresh lemon juice
- 2 cups chilled water

Instructions:

1. Add all the ingredients in a high-power blender and pulse until creamy and smooth.
2. Pour the smoothie into two glasses and serve immediately.

Nutritional Information per Serving:

Calories	: 44
Fat	: 0.8g
Saturated Fat	: 0.3g
Carbohydrates	: 8.5g
Fiber	: 2.7g
Sugar	: 2.6g
Protein	: 2.7g
Sodium	: 39mg

Green Sunflower Butter Smoothie

 Servings: 2

Preparation Time: 10 minutes

Ingredients:

- 1 avocado, peeled, pitted and chopped
- 2 cups fresh spinach
- 1 scoop unflavored collagen protein powder
- 1 tablespoon sunflower seed butter
- 1 teaspoon vanilla extract
- ½ tablespoon MCT oil
- 1 cup unsweetened almond milk
- 1 cup ice cubes

Instructions:

1. Add all the ingredients in a high-power blender and pulse until creamy and smooth.
2. Pour the smoothie into two glasses and serve immediately.

Nutritional Information per Serving:

Calories	: 282
Fat	: 25.8g
Saturated Fat	: 7.6g
Carbohydrates	: 11.9g
Fiber	: 6.9g
Sugar	: 0.8g
Protein	: 5.6g
Sodium	: 126mg

Chapter 4: Plant-Based Smoothie & Juicing Recipes

Baby Greens Smoothie

Servings: 2

Preparation Time: 10 minutes

Ingredients:

- 1½ cups fresh baby spinach
- 1½ cups fresh baby kale
- 1 tablespoon almond butter
- 1 tablespoon chia seeds
- 1/8 teaspoon ground cinnamon
- Pinch of ground cloves
- 1½ cups unsweetened almond milk
- ½ cup ice cubes

Instructions:

1. Add all the ingredients in a high-power blender and pulse until creamy and smooth.
2. Pour the smoothie into two glasses and serve immediately.

Nutritional Information per Serving:

Calories	: 208
Fat	: 18.7g
Saturated Fat	: 7.5g
Carbohydrates	: 9.1g
Fiber	: 3.5g
Sugar	: 0.4g
Protein	: 5g
Sodium	: 129mg

Green Veggies Smoothie

Servings: 2

Preparation Time: 10 minutes

Ingredients:

- 1 cup fresh spinach
- ¼ cup broccoli florets, chopped
- ¼ cup green cabbage, chopped
- ½ of small green bell pepper, seeded and chopped
- 2 cups chilled water

Instructions:

1. Add all the ingredients in a high-power blender and pulse until creamy and smooth.
2. Pour the smoothie into two glasses and serve immediately.

Nutritional Information per Serving:

Calories	: 19
Fat	: 0.2g
Saturated Fat	: 0g
Carbohydrates	: 4.1g
Fiber	: 1.3g
Sugar	: 2g
Protein	: 1.2g
Sodium	: 18mg

The Plant-Based Vegan: Juicing and Smoothie Diet Cookbook
200 Delicious Smoothie & Juicing Recipes To Lose Weight, Detox Your Body, and Live A Long Healthy Life

Digestive Improvement Smoothies

Our digestive system has various organs and glands working in harmony to make digestion and absorption of nutrients possible. Inside our gut system, there are friendly bacteria that aids digestion. Food used in these smoothies supports the gut biome and improves internal gut health by providing necessary probiotics. Other nutrients present in these smoothies can speed up the digestion process by managing the release of enzymes and hormones.

Chapter 4: Plant-Based Smoothie & Juicing Recipes

Blueberry & Beet Smoothie

 Servings: 2

Preparation Time: 10 minutes

Ingredients:

- ¾ cup frozen blueberries
- ½ frozen banana, peeled
- 1 small beet, trimmed, peeled and cut into chunks
- 1 Medjool date, pitted
- 2 tablespoons fresh lime juice
- 2 tablespoons ground flaxseed
- Pinch of sea salt
- ¾ cup unsweetened almond milk
- ½ cup ice cubes

Instructions:

1. Add all the ingredients in a high-power blender and pulse until creamy and smooth.
2. Pour the smoothie into two glasses and serve immediately.

Nutritional Information per Serving:

Calories	: 173
Fat	: 3.9g
Saturated Fat	: 0.5g
Carbohydrates	: 33g
Fiber	: 6.4g
Sugar	: 22.1g
Protein	: 3.8g
Sodium	: 186mg

Blueberry & Pineapple Smoothie

 Servings: 2

Preparation Time: 10 minutes

Ingredients:

- 1 cup fresh blueberries
- 1½ cups fresh pineapple chunks
- 1 frozen banana, peeled
- 2 tablespoons fresh mint leaves
- ½ cup fresh orange juice
- 1 cup unsweetened almond milk
- ½ cup ice cubes

Instructions:

1. Add all the ingredients in a high-power blender and pulse until creamy and smooth.
2. Pour the smoothie into two glasses and serve immediately.

Nutritional Information per Serving:

Calories	: 206
Fat	: 2.5g
Saturated Fat	: 0.3g
Carbohydrates	: 48.2g
Fiber	: 6g
Sugar	: 31.8g
Protein	: 3g
Sodium	: 95mg

Chapter 4: Plant-Based Smoothie & Juicing Recipes

Pineapple Smoothie

Servings: 2

Preparation Time: 10 minutes

Ingredients:

- 1 cup frozen pineapple chunks
- 1 large frozen banana
- ¼ cup fresh parsley leaves
- 1 teaspoon fresh ginger, grated
- ½ cup coconut water
- 1 cup water

Instructions:

1. Add all the ingredients in a high-power blender and pulse until creamy and smooth.
2. Pour the smoothie into two glasses and serve immediately.

Nutritional Information per Serving:

Calories	: 119
Fat	: 0.6g
Saturated Fat	: 0.2g
Carbohydrates	: 29.7g
Fiber	: 3.9g
Sugar	: 18.1g
Protein	: 1.9g
Sodium	: 69mg

Pear Smoothie

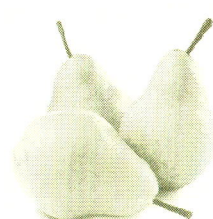

Servings: 2

Preparation Time: 10 minutes

Ingredients:

- 2 pears, cored and sliced
- ½ cup old-fashioned rolled oats
- 1 tablespoon maple syrup
- ¼ teaspoon ground cardamom
- 1½ cups unsweetened almond milk
- ½ cup ice cubes

Instructions:

1. Add all the ingredients in a high-power blender and pulse until creamy and smooth.
2. Pour the smoothie into two glasses and serve immediately.

Nutritional Information per Serving:

Calories	: 253
Fat	: 4.3g
Saturated Fat	: 0.5g
Carbohydrates	: 53.7g
Fiber	: 9.3g
Sugar	: 26.5g
Protein	: 4.2g
Sodium	: 139mg

Chapter 4: Plant-Based Smoothie & Juicing Recipes

Peach Smoothie

 Servings: 2

 Preparation Time: 10 minutes

Ingredients:

- 1 frozen banana, peeled and chopped
- 1 cup frozen peaches, pitted and chopped
- 1 tablespoon chia seeds
- 1 teaspoon ground cinnamon
- ½ teaspoon ground ginger
- 1 teaspoon maple syrup
- 1½ cups unsweetened almond milk

Instructions:

1. Add all the ingredients in a high-power blender and pulse until creamy and smooth.
2. Pour the smoothie into two glasses and serve immediately.

Nutritional Information per Serving:

Calories	: 140
Fat	: 4.3g
Saturated Fat	: 0.4g
Carbohydrates	: 27g
Fiber	: 5.4g
Sugar	: 16.2g
Protein	: 2.9g
Sodium	: 136mg

Peach, Pear & Papaya Smoothie

 Servings: 2

 **Preparation Time:** 10 minutes

Ingredients:

- ¾ cup papaya, peeled and chopped
- ¾ cup peaches, pitted and chopped
- ½ cup pear, peeled, cored and chopped
- 1 teaspoon fresh ginger, peeled and chopped
- 2 fresh mint leaves
- 1 cup coconut water
- 1 cup ice, crushed

Instructions:

1. Add all the ingredients in a high-power blender and pulse until creamy and smooth.
2. Pour the smoothie into two glasses and serve immediately.

Nutritional Information per Serving:

Calories	: 392
Fat	: 20.2g
Saturated Fat	: 0g
Carbohydrates	: 51g
Fiber	: 9.8g
Sugar	: 2.3g
Protein	: 2.6g
Sodium	: 0mg

Chapter 4: Plant-Based Smoothie & Juicing Recipes

Papaya Smoothie

Servings: 2

Preparation Time: 10 minutes

Ingredients:

- 2 cups papaya, peeled and sliced
- 1½ cups unsweetened almond milk
- ½ cup ice cubes

Instructions:

1. Add all the ingredients in a high-power blender and pulse until creamy and smooth.
2. Pour the smoothie into two glasses and serve immediately.

Nutritional Information per Serving:

Calories	: 82
Fat	: 2.2g
Saturated Fat	: 0.3g
Carbohydrates	: 16.7g
Fiber	: 3g
Sugar	: 11.3g
Protein	: 1.2g
Sodium	: 102mg

Papaya & Carrot Smoothie

 Servings: 2

 Preparation Time: 10 minutes

Ingredients:

- 1½ cups papaya, peeled and chopped
- 1 cup carrot, trimmed, peeled and chopped
- 2 dates, pitted
- 1 tablespoon fresh lemon juice
- 1½ cups coconut water
- ¼ cup ice cubes

Instructions:

1. Add all the ingredients in a high-power blender and pulse until creamy and smooth.
2. Pour the smoothie into two glasses and serve immediately.

Nutritional Information per Serving:

Calories	: 128
Fat	: 0.8g
Saturated Fat	: 0.5g
Carbohydrates	: 30.3g
Fiber	: 5.9g
Sugar	: 21.3g
Protein	: 2.5g
Sodium	: 238mg

Chapter 4: Plant-Based Smoothie & Juicing Recipes

Carrot & Orange Smoothie

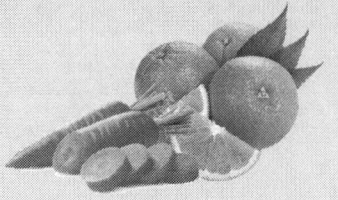

Servings: 2

Preparation Time: 10 minutes

Ingredients:

- 2 oranges, peeled, seeded and sectioned
- 1 carrot, trimmed, peeled and chopped
- 2 bananas, peeled
- 1 (1-inch) piece fresh ginger root, peeled
- 1 cup chilled water

Instructions:

1. Add all the ingredients in a high-power blender and pulse until creamy and smooth.
2. Pour the smoothie into two glasses and serve immediately.

Nutritional Information per Serving:

Calories	: 205
Fat	: 0.6g
Saturated Fat	: 0.2g
Carbohydrates	: 51.7g
Fiber	: 8.3g
Sugar	: 33.2g
Protein	: 3.3g
Sodium	: 22mg

Green Date Smoothie

Servings: 2

Preparation Time: 10 minutes

Ingredients:

- 1 avocado, peeled, peeled, pitted and sliced
- 1 cup frozen spinach
- ½ cup frozen cauliflower florets
- ½ tablespoon ground flaxseed
- 1 Medjool date, pitted
- 1½ cups unsweetened almond milk

Instructions:

1. Add all the ingredients in a high-power blender and pulse until creamy and smooth.
2. Pour the smoothie into two glasses and serve immediately.

Nutritional Information per Serving:

Calories	: 294
Fat	: 22.9g
Saturated Fat	: 4.4g
Carbohydrates	: 23g
Fiber	: 9.9g
Sugar	: 10.2g
Protein	: 4.4g
Sodium	: 161mg

The Plant-Based Vegan: Juicing and Smoothie Diet Cookbook
200 Delicious Smoothie & Juicing Recipes To Lose Weight, Detox Your Body, and Live A Long Healthy Life

High-Energy Smoothies

These smoothies are rich in super-foods that are packed with energy. Instead of providing empty calories, these smoothies offer healthy energy through the unsaturated fatty acids present in nuts and seeds, proteins from nut-based milk, super-food and protein powders and carbohydrates from juicy fruits. These energizing smoothies are great for people involved in extreme physical activities; having these smoothies can instantly provide their cells with enough energy to carry out metabolism quickly.

Chapter 4: Plant-Based Smoothie & Juicing Recipes

Date & Almond Smoothie

 Servings: 2

 Preparation Time: 10 minutes

Ingredients:

- 1 cup Medjool dates, pitted and chopped
- ½ cup almonds, chopped
- 1½ cups unsweetened almond milk
- ¼ cup ice cubes

Instructions:

1. Add all the ingredients in a high-power blender and pulse until creamy and smooth.
2. Pour the smoothie into two glasses and serve immediately.

Nutritional Information per Serving:

Calories	: 418
Fat	: 14.9g
Saturated Fat	: 1.2g
Carbohydrates	: 73.4g
Fiber	: 10.8g
Sugar	: 57.4g
Protein	: 8g
Sodium	: 137mg

Nutty Banana Smoothie

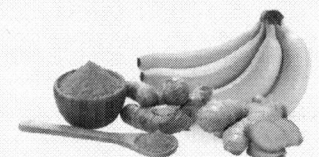

 Servings: 2

 Preparation Time: 10 minutes

Ingredients:

- 1 frozen banana, peeled and sliced
- 1 (¼-inch) piece fresh turmeric root, grated
- 1 (½-inch) piece fresh ginger root, peeled and chopped
- ½ cup pecans, chopped
- ½ cup walnuts, chopped
- 1 tablespoon chia seeds
- 1 tablespoon fresh maca powder
- ½ teaspoon ground cinnamon
- 1½ cups unsweetened almond milk

Instructions:

1. Add all the ingredients in a high-power blender and pulse until creamy and smooth.
2. Pour the smoothie into two glasses and serve immediately.

Nutritional Information per Serving:

Calories	: 522
Fat	: 44.8g
Saturated Fat	: 3.7g
Carbohydrates	: 26.8g
Fiber	: 10g
Sugar	: 9.2g
Protein	: 9.2g
Sodium	: 137mg

Banana Peanut Butter Smoothie

Servings: 2

Preparation Time: 10 minutes

Ingredients:

- 2 cups frozen bananas, peeled and sliced
- 2 tablespoons all-natural peanut butter
- 2 tablespoon ground flaxseeds
- 1 teaspoon vanilla extract
- ½ cup plain coconut yogurt
- 1 cup unsweetened almond milk

Instructions:

1. Add all the ingredients in a high-power blender and pulse until creamy and smooth.
2. Pour the smoothie into two glasses and serve immediately.

Nutritional Information per Serving:

Calories	: 322
Fat	: 14.5g
Saturated Fat	: 3.9g
Carbohydrates	: 43.5g
Fiber	: 9.3g
Sugar	: 20.2g
Protein	: 8.4g
Sodium	: 144mg

Raspberry Peanut Butter Smoothie

Servings: 2

Preparation Time: 10 minutes

Ingredients:

- 1 banana, peeled and sliced
- 2 cups fresh raspberries
- 2 tablespoons peanut butter
- 1 tablespoon chia seeds
- 1 tablespoon maple syrup
- 1 scoop soy protein powder
- 1½ cups unsweetened almond milk
- ¼ cup ice cubes

Instructions:

1. Add all the ingredients in a high-power blender and pulse until creamy and smooth.
2. Pour the smoothie into two glasses and serve immediately.

Nutritional Information per Serving:

Calories	: 340
Fat	: 13.5g
Saturated Fat	: 2.1g
Carbohydrates	: 41g
Fiber	: 12.5g
Sugar	: 20.1g
Protein	: 20.8g
Sodium	: 211mg

Chapter 4: Plant-Based Smoothie & Juicing Recipes

Berries Smoothie

Ingredients:

- 2 cups mixed fresh berries
- 1 tablespoon MCT oil
- ½ teaspoon vanilla extract
- 3-5 drops liquid stevia
- ¾ cup coconut cream
- 1 cup unsweetened almond milk
- ¼ cup ice cubes

Instructions:

1. Add all the ingredients in a high-power blender and pulse until creamy and smooth.
2. Pour the smoothie into two glasses and serve immediately.

Servings: 2
Preparation Time: 10 minutes

Nutritional Information per Serving:

Calories	: 375
Fat	: 30.7g
Saturated Fat	: 26.2g
Carbohydrates	: 23.1g
Fiber	: 7.5g
Sugar	: 13.1g
Protein	: 3.6g
Sodium	: 104mg

Kiwi & Melon Smoothie

Ingredients:

- 2 kiwi fruit, peeled and chopped
- 1 cup melon, peeled and chopped
- ½ teaspoon fresh ginger, chopped
- 1½ scoops unsweetened protein powder
- ½ tablespoon fresh lime juice
- 1¾ cups fresh green grape juice
- ¼ cup ice cubes

Instructions:

1. Add all the ingredients in a high-power blender and pulse until creamy and smooth.
2. Pour the smoothie into two glasses and serve immediately.

Servings: 2
Preparation Time: 10 minutes

Nutritional Information per Serving:

Calories	: 314
Fat	: 1.8g
Saturated Fat	: 0.1g
Carbohydrates	: 53.8g
Fiber	: 3.4g
Sugar	: 48.5g
Protein	: 22.7g
Sodium	: 217mg

Chapter 4: Plant-Based Smoothie & Juicing Recipes

Sweet Potato & Orange Smoothie

Servings: 2

Preparation Time: 10 minutes

Ingredients:

- 1 large frozen banana, peeled and sliced
- 1 cup sweet potato puree
- 1 teaspoon fresh ginger, chopped
- 1 tablespoon flaxseeds meal
- 1 tablespoon coconut butter
- ¼ teaspoon ground turmeric
- ¼ teaspoon ground cinnamon
- 1 cup unsweetened coconut milk
- ¼ cup fresh orange juice
- ¼ cup ice cubes

Instructions:

1. Add all the ingredients in a high-power blender and pulse until creamy and smooth.
2. Pour the smoothie into two glasses and serve immediately.

Nutritional Information per Serving:

Calories	: 420
Fat	: 23g
Saturated Fat	: 19.3g
Carbohydrates	: 46.8g
Fiber	: 7.9g
Sugar	: 20.9g
Protein	: 6.1g
Sodium	: 77mg

Pumpkin & Banana Smoothie

Servings: 2

Preparation Time: 10 minutes

Ingredients:

- ¾ cup pumpkin puree
- 2 medium frozen bananas, peeled and sliced
- ½ teaspoon pumpkin pie spice
- 2 scoops unsweetened vegan protein powder
- 4-6 drops liquid stevia
- 1½ cups unsweetened coconut milk

Instructions:

1. Add all the ingredients in a high-power blender and pulse until creamy and smooth.
2. Pour the smoothie into two glasses and serve immediately.

Nutritional Information per Serving:

Calories	: 524
Fat	: 26.5g
Saturated Fat	: 22.8g
Carbohydrates	: 39.2g
Fiber	: 5.8g
Sugar	: 22g
Protein	: 29.9g
Sodium	: 326mg

Chapter 4: Plant-Based Smoothie & Juicing Recipes

Matcha, Spinach & Pineapple Smoothie

 Servings: 2

Preparation Time: 10 minutes

Ingredients:

- 1 cup frozen pineapple
- 1 banana, peeled and sliced
- 1 cup fresh baby spinach
- ½ of avocado, peeled, pitted and chopped
- 1 tablespoon coconut oil
- 1 teaspoon matcha green tea powder
- ½ cup fresh orange juice
- 1 cup unsweetened almond milk

Instructions:

1. Add all the ingredients in a high-power blender and pulse until creamy and smooth.
2. Pour the smoothie into two glasses and serve immediately.

Nutritional Information per Serving:

Calories	: 307
Fat	: 18.8g
Saturated Fat	: 8.2g
Carbohydrates	: 36.8g
Fiber	: 7g
Sugar	: 20.9g
Protein	: 3.5g
Sodium	: 107mg

Greens & Carrot Smoothie

 Servings: 2

 Preparation Time: 10 minutes

Ingredients:

- 1 large banana, peeled and sliced
- 1 cup fresh baby kale
- 1 cup fresh baby spinach
- 1 tablespoon almond butter
- 1 scoop unsweetened vegan protein powder
- 2 tablespoons raw wheat germ, toasted
- ¼ teaspoon ground cinnamon
- 2 teaspoons flax oil
- 1½ cups fresh carrot juice
- ¼ cup ice cubes

Instructions:

1. Add all the ingredients in a high-power blender and pulse until creamy and smooth.
2. Pour the smoothie into two glasses and serve immediately.

Nutritional Information per Serving:

Calories	: 302
Fat	: 13.1g
Saturated Fat	: 1.1g
Carbohydrates	: 31.1g
Fiber	: 7.6g
Sugar	: 13.5g
Protein	: 19.1g
Sodium	: 288mg

Green Smoothies

Prepared using a blend of a variety of green vegetables and some fruits juices, these smoothies are the reservoirs of essential minerals and antioxidants. Anyone aiming to improve their digestive system, boost immunity and cleanse blood should consume these green smoothies. These smoothies are low in calories and carbs, and for this reason, they are considered effective for weight loss or weight management as well.

Chapter 4: Plant-Based Smoothie & Juicing Recipes

Mint Smoothie

Servings: 2

Preparation Time: 10 minutes

Ingredients:

- 1 cup mint leaves
- 2 large frozen bananas, peeled and sliced
- 1 tablespoon hemp seeds
- 1½ cups unsweetened almond milk

Instructions:

1. Add all the ingredients in a high-power blender and pulse until creamy and smooth.
2. Pour the smoothie into two glasses and serve immediately.

Nutritional Information per Serving:

Calories	: 192
Fat	: 5.1g
Saturated Fat	: 0.6g
Carbohydrates	: 36.6g
Fiber	: 7.5g
Sugar	: 16.6g
Protein	: 5g
Sodium	: 150mg

Avocado Smoothie

Servings: 2

Preparation Time: 10 minutes

Ingredients:

- 1 large avocado, peeled, pitted and chopped
- 1 teaspoon lime zest, grated freshly
- 1-2 tablespoons maple syrup
- 1 tablespoon fresh lime juice
- 1½ cups filtered water
- ¼ cup ice cubes

Instructions:

1. Add all the ingredients in a high-power blender and pulse until creamy and smooth.
2. Pour the smoothie into two glasses and serve immediately.

Nutritional Information per Serving:

Calories	: 232
Fat	: 19.6g
Saturated Fat	: 4.1g
Carbohydrates	: 15.6g
Fiber	: 6.8g
Sugar	: 6.5g
Protein	: 1.9g
Sodium	: 7mg

Chapter 4: Plant-Based Smoothie & Juicing Recipes

Grapes & Swiss Chard Smoothie

Servings: 2

Preparation Time: 10 minutes

Ingredients:

- 2 cups seedless green grapes
- 2 cups fresh Swiss chard, trimmed and chopped
- 2 tablespoons maple syrup
- 1 teaspoon fresh lemon juice
- 1½ cups water
- ¼ cup ice cubes

Instructions:

1. Place all the ingredients in a high-speed blender and pulse until creamy and smooth.
2. Pour the smoothie into two glasses and serve immediately.

Nutritional Information per Serving:

Calories	: 176
Fat	: 0.2g
Saturated Fat	: 0g
Carbohydrates	: 44.9g
Fiber	: 1.7g
Sugar	: 37.9g
Protein	: 0.7g
Sodium	: 83mg

Pear & Spinach Smoothie

Servings: 2

Preparation Time: 10 minutes

Ingredients:

- 1 pear, peeled, cored and sliced
- 1 banana, peeled and sliced
- 2 cups fresh spinach
- ½ cup chilled coconut water
- ½ cup chilled filtered water

Instructions:

1. Add all the ingredients in a high-power blender and pulse until creamy and smooth.
2. Pour the smoothie into two glasses and serve immediately.

Nutritional Information per Serving:

Calories	: 111
Fat	: 0.5g
Saturated Fat	: 0.2g
Carbohydrates	: 27.4g
Fiber	: 5g
Sugar	: 15.7g
Protein	: 2.2g
Sodium	: 88mg

Chapter 4: Plant-Based Smoothie & Juicing Recipes

Apple & Avocado Smoothie

Servings: 2

Preparation Time: 10 minutes

Ingredients:

- 1 large green apple, peeled, cored and sliced
- 1 avocado, peeled, pitted and chopped
- 4-6 drops liquid stevia
- 2 cups chilled filtered water

Instructions:

1. Add all the ingredients in a high-power blender and pulse until creamy and smooth.
2. Pour the smoothie into two glasses and serve immediately.

Nutritional Information per Serving:

Calories	: 263
Fat	: 19.8g
Saturated Fat	: 4.1g
Carbohydrates	: 24g
Fiber	: 9.4g
Sugar	: 12.1g
Protein	: 2.2g
Sodium	: 7mg

Lemon Kale Smoothie

Servings: 2

Preparation Time: 10 minutes

Ingredients:

- 2 cups fresh kale leaves
- 1 large banana, peeled and sliced
- 2 tablespoons fresh lemon juice
- 1½ cups unsweetened almond milk
- ¼ cup ice cubes

Instructions:

1. Add all the ingredients in a high-power blender and pulse until creamy and smooth.
2. Pour the smoothie into two glasses and serve immediately.

Nutritional Information per Serving:

Calories	: 109
Fat	: 3.2g
Saturated Fat	: 0.4g
Carbohydrates	: 19.8g
Fiber	: 3.3g
Sugar	: 7.5g
Protein	: 3g
Sodium	: 156mg

The Plant-Based Vegan: Juicing and Smoothie Diet Cookbook
200 Delicious Smoothie & Juicing Recipes To Lose Weight, Detox Your Body, and Live A Long Healthy Life

Kiwi, Grapes & Kale Smoothie

Servings: 2

Preparation Time: 10 minutes

Ingredients:

- 2 kiwi fruit, peeled and chopped
- 1 cup seedless green grapes
- 2 cups fresh kale, trimmed and chopped
- 1 tablespoon maple syrup
- ½ tablespoon fresh lime juice
- 1½ cups filtered water
- ¼ cup ice cubes

Instructions:

1. Add all the ingredients in a high-power blender and pulse until creamy and smooth.
2. Pour the smoothie into two glasses and serve immediately.

Nutritional Information per Serving:

Calories	: 164
Fat	: 0.4g
Saturated Fat	: 0g
Carbohydrates	: 40g
Fiber	: 3.8g
Sugar	: 25.6g
Protein	: 2.9g
Sodium	: 34mg

Green Fruity Smoothie

Servings: 2

Preparation Time: 10 minutes

Ingredients:

- 1 cup frozen mango, peeled, pitted and chopped
- 1 large frozen banana, peeled
- 2 cups fresh baby spinach
- 1 scoop unsweetened vegan vanilla protein powder
- ¼ cup pumpkin seeds
- 2 tablespoons hemp hearts
- 1½ cups unsweetened almond milk

Instructions:

1. In a high-speed blender, place all the ingredients and pulse until creamy and smooth.
2. Pour into two glasses and serve immediately.

Nutritional Information per Serving:

Calories	: 355
Fat	: 16.1g
Saturated Fat	: 2.4g
Carbohydrates	: 34.6g
Fiber	: 6.2g
Sugar	: 19.9g
Protein	: 2.9g
Sodium	: 295mg

Chapter 4: Plant-Based Smoothie & Juicing Recipes

Cucumber & Lettuce Smoothie

 Servings: 2

 Preparation Time: 10 minutes

Ingredients:

- 1 cucumber, peeled and chopped
- 1 cup lettuce leaves
- ½ cup fresh mint leaves
- 1 tablespoon fresh ginger, grated
- 2 cups coconut water
- 1 tablespoon fresh lime juice
- ¼ cup ice cubes

Instructions:

1. Add all the ingredients in a high-power blender and pulse until creamy and smooth.
2. Pour the smoothie into two glasses and serve immediately.

Nutritional Information per Serving:

Calories	: 92
Fat	: 1g
Saturated Fat	: 0.6g
Carbohydrates	: 40g
Fiber	: 3.8g
Sugar	: 25.6g
Protein	: 2.9g
Sodium	: 34mg

Lettuce & Avocado Smoothie

 Servings: 2

Preparation Time: 10 minutes

Ingredients:

- 1½ cups romaine lettuce leaves, chopped
- 1 cup avocado, peeled, pitted and chopped
- ¼ cup fresh mint leaves
- 2 teaspoons flaxseed meal
- 3-4 drops liquid stevia
- 1½ cups filtered water
- ½ cup ice cubes

Instructions:

1. Add all the ingredients in a high-power blender and pulse until creamy and smooth.
2. Pour the smoothie into two glasses and serve immediately.

Nutritional Information per Serving:

Calories	: 157
Fat	: 15.1g
Saturated Fat	: 3.1g
Carbohydrates	: 8.1g
Fiber	: 6.3g
Sugar	: 0.5g
Protein	: 2.3g
Sodium	: 9mg

Healthy Skin Smoothies

Skin being the largest organ of the body, requires most of the care. Whatever we consume through our diet reflect the health of our skin. Having smoothies rich in anti-Oxidants and healthy vitamins can drastically improve skin health. These smoothies have nutrients that aid collagen production in the skin and make for elasticity and younger-looking. Vitamin C, for example, plays an important role in collagen production in the skin, so having fruits rich in Vitamin C through the use of these smoothies will help give you healthier looking skin.

Chapter 4: Plant-Based Smoothie & Juicing Recipes

Peach & Aloe Vera Smoothie

Servings: 2
Preparation Time: 10 minutes

Ingredients:

- 1 large peach, peeled, pitted, and chopped
- 1 medium frozen banana, peeled and sliced
- 2 ounces aloe vera
- ½ teaspoon fresh ginger, peeled and chopped
- 2 tablespoons flaxseeds
- ½ teaspoon vanilla extract
- 1¾ cups unsweetened almond milk

Instructions:

1. Add all the ingredients in a high-powered blender and pulse until creamy and smooth.
2. Pour the smoothie into two glasses and serve immediately.

Nutritional Information per Serving:

Calories	: 162
Fat	: 5.7g
Saturated Fat	: 0.6g
Carbohydrates	: 25.7g
Fiber	: 5.5g
Sugar	: 14.5g
Protein	: 3.6g
Sodium	: 160mg

Orange, Kiwi & Carrot Smoothie

Servings: 2
Preparation Time: 10 minutes

Ingredients:

- 1 cup kiwi, peeled and chopped roughly
- 2 carrots, peeled and sliced
- 3 tablespoons cashews
- ½ cup fresh orange juice
- 1½ cups unsweetened almond milk
- ¼ cup ice cubes

Instructions:

1. Add all the ingredients in a high-powered blender and pulse until creamy and smooth.
2. Pour the smoothie into two glasses and serve immediately.

Nutritional Information per Serving:

Calories	: 211
Fat	: 9.2g
Saturated Fat	: 1.5g
Carbohydrates	: 31.1g
Fiber	: 5.4g
Sugar	: 16.8g
Protein	: 4.7g
Sodium	: 182mg

The Plant-Based Vegan: Juicing and Smoothie Diet Cookbook
200 Delicious Smoothie & Juicing Recipes To Lose Weight, Detox Your Body, and Live A Long Healthy Life

Chapter 4: Plant-Based Smoothie & Juicing Recipes

Sweet Potato & Mango Smoothie

Servings: 2

Preparation Time: 10 minutes

Ingredients:

- 1 cup boiled sweet potato, peeled and sliced
- 1 cup mango, peeled, pitted and chopped
- ¼ cup fresh orange juice
- 1½ cups filtered water
- ½ cup ice cubes

Instructions:

1. Add all the ingredients in a high-powered blender and pulse until creamy and smooth.
2. Pour the smoothie into two glasses and serve immediately.

Nutritional Information per Serving:

Calories	: 154
Fat	: 0.6g
Saturated Fat	: 0.1g
Carbohydrates	: 36.3g
Fiber	: 4.7g
Sugar	: 20.4g
Protein	: 2.9g
Sodium	: 37mg

Sweet Potato & Carrot Smoothie

Servings: 2

Preparation Time: 10 minutes

Ingredients:

- 1 large carrots, peeled and chopped
- 2 celery stalks
- 1 cup boiled sweet potato, peeled and chopped
- 1 teaspoon fresh ginger root, peeled and chopped
- 1½ cups filtered water
- ½ cup ice cubes

Instructions:

1. Add all the ingredients in a high-powered blender and pulse until creamy and smooth.
2. Pour the smoothie into two glasses and serve immediately.

Nutritional Information per Serving:

Calories	: 108
Fat	: 0.2g
Saturated Fat	: 0g
Carbohydrates	: 24.9g
Fiber	: 4.5g
Sugar	: 8.5g
Protein	: 2.5g
Sodium	: 74mg

Chapter 4: Plant-Based Smoothie & Juicing Recipes

Raspberry Date Smoothie

 Servings: 2

 Preparation Time: 10 minutes

Ingredients:

- 2 cups frozen raspberries
- 1 banana, peeled and sliced
- 6 dates, pitted
- 1 tablespoon flaxseeds
- 1¾ cups filtered water

Instructions:

1. Add all the ingredients in a high-powered blender and pulse until creamy and smooth.
2. Pour the smoothie into two glasses and serve immediately.

Nutritional Information per Serving:

Calories	: 205
Fat	: 2.2g
Saturated Fat	: 0.3g
Carbohydrates	: 47.9g
Fiber	: 12.5g
Sugar	: 28.5g
Protein	: 3.4g
Sodium	: 3mg

Mango & Cashew Smoothie

 Servings: 2

 Preparation Time: 10 minutes

Ingredients:

- 1 medium frozen banana, peeled
- 1 cup frozen mango chunks
- ¼ cup cashews, chopped
- 1 tablespoon chia seeds
- 1 tablespoon maple syrup
- ½ teaspoon vanilla extract
- ½ teaspoon ground cardamom
- ¼ teaspoon ground turmeric
- 1/8 teaspoon ground ginger
- 1 cup coconut water

Instructions:

1. Add all the ingredients in a high-powered blender and pulse until creamy and smooth.
2. Pour the smoothie into two glasses and serve immediately.

Nutritional Information per Serving:

Calories	: 270
Fat	: 10g
Saturated Fat	: 2g
Carbohydrates	: 44.8g
Fiber	: 6.1g
Sugar	: 28.6g
Protein	: 5.6g
Sodium	: 131mg

Chapter 4: Plant-Based Smoothie & Juicing Recipes

Mixed Fruit Smoothie

Servings: 2

Preparation Time: 10 minutes

Ingredients:

- 1 cup frozen strawberries
- 1 kiwi, peeled
- 1 apple, peeled, cored and chopped roughly
- 1 large frozen banana, peeled and sliced
- 1 tablespoon ground flaxseed
- 1 tablespoon fresh lemon juice
- 1½ cups unsweetened almond milk

Instructions:

1. Add all the ingredients in a high-powered blender and pulse until creamy and smooth.
2. Pour the smoothie into two glasses and serve immediately.

Nutritional Information per Serving:

Calories	: 215
Fat	: 4.6g
Saturated Fat	: 0.5g
Carbohydrates	: 44.7g
Fiber	: 8.8g
Sugar	: 27.1g
Protein	: 3.4g
Sodium	: 141mg

Tomato Smoothie

Servings: 2

Preparation Time: 10 minutes

Ingredients:

- 5 medium tomatoes
- 5-6 fresh basil leaves
- 2 teaspoons coconut oil
- 1½ cups fresh orange juice
- ¼ cup ice cubes

Instructions:

1. Add all the ingredients in a high-powered blender and pulse until creamy and smooth.
2. Pour the smoothie into two glasses and serve immediately.

Nutritional Information per Serving:

Calories	: 179
Fat	: 5.5g
Saturated Fat	: 4.1g
Carbohydrates	: 31.3g
Fiber	: 4.1g
Sugar	: 23.7g
Protein	: 4g
Sodium	: 17mg

The Plant-Based Vegan: Juicing and Smoothie Diet Cookbook
200 Delicious Smoothie & Juicing Recipes To Lose Weight, Detox Your Body, and Live A Long Healthy Life

Chapter 4: Plant-Based Smoothie & Juicing Recipes

Fruity Spinach & Lettuce Smoothie

Servings: 2

Preparation Time: 10 minutes

Ingredients:

- 1 small green apple, cored and chopped
- 1 small pear, cored and chopped
- 1 medium banana, peeled and cut in thirds
- 1 cup fresh spinach
- 1 cup romaine lettuce, chopped
- 1 cups celery, chopped
- ½ cup fresh parsley
- 2 tablespoons fresh lemon juice
- 2 cups chilled filtered water

Instructions:

1. Add all the ingredients in a high-powered blender and pulse until creamy and smooth.
2. Pour the smoothie into two glasses and serve immediately.

Nutritional Information per Serving:

Calories	: 175
Fat	: 0.9g
Saturated Fat	: 0.2g
Carbohydrates	: 43.6g
Fiber	: 8.3g
Sugar	: 27.1g
Protein	: 2.7g
Sodium	: 68mg

Kale, Avocado & Fruit Smoothie

Servings: 2

Preparation Time: 10 minutes

Ingredients:

- 1 frozen banana, peeled and sliced
- 1 cup frozen pineapple chunks
- 1 cup frozen mango chunks
- 2 cups fresh spinach
- ½ avocado, peeled, pitted and sliced
- 1 tablespoon ground flaxseed
- 1 cup coconut water

Instructions:

1. Add all the ingredients in a high-powered blender and pulse until creamy and smooth.
2. Pour the smoothie into two glasses and serve immediately.

Nutritional Information per Serving:

Calories	: 290
Fat	: 12.4g
Saturated Fat	: 3.9g
Carbohydrates	: 46.7g
Fiber	: 9.4g
Sugar	: 30.1g
Protein	: 4.6g
Sodium	: 156mg

The Plant-Based Vegan: Juicing and Smoothie Diet Cookbook
200 Delicious Smoothie & Juicing Recipes To Lose Weight, Detox Your Body, and Live A Long Healthy Life

Kid-Friendly Smoothies

Growing bones and muscles of the kids need a good amount of all the macro and micronutrients. Minerals like calcium are good for the bones, and vitamins A, C and D are essential to support their growth. Keeping these needs in mind, these kid-friendly smoothies are specially created for young ones. Not only are these smoothies healthy for their bodies, but they also offer good taste and tempting flavors so that the kids would love to have these smoothies. They are great for the kids who otherwise don't enjoy eating fruits and vegetables; in this way, you can incorporate all the healthy ingredients into you're their diet.

Banana Smoothie

 Servings: 2

 Preparation Time: 10 minutes

Ingredients:

- 2 large frozen bananas, peeled and sliced
- 2 tablespoons almond butter
- 1 scoop unsweetened vegan protein powder
- ¼ teaspoon vanilla extract
- 1½ cups unsweetened almond milk

Instructions:

1. Add all the ingredients in a high-powered blender and pulse until creamy and smooth.
2. Pour the smoothie into two glasses and serve immediately.

Nutritional Information per Serving:

Calories	: 293
Fat	: 12.6g
Saturated Fat	: 1.1g
Carbohydrates	: 31.5g
Fiber	: 5.4g
Sugar	: 15.2g
Protein	: 18.1g
Sodium	: 269mg

Pistachio Banana Smoothie

 Servings: 2

 Preparation Time: 10 minutes

Ingredients:

- 2 large frozen bananas, peeled and sliced
- ¼ cup pistachios, chopped
- 1½ cups unsweetened almond milk

Instructions:

1. Add all the ingredients in a high-powered blender and pulse until creamy and smooth.
2. Pour the smoothie into two glasses and serve immediately.

Nutritional Information per Serving:

Calories	: 191
Fat	: 6.6g
Saturated Fat	: 0.8g
Carbohydrates	: 34.6g
Fiber	: 5g
Sugar	: 17.1g
Protein	: 3.7g
Sodium	: 176mg

Mango & Walnut Smoothie

Servings: 2

Preparation Time: 10 minutes

Ingredients:

- 1 medium mango, peeled, pitted and chopped
- 1 large banana, peeled and sliced
- ¼ cup walnuts, chopped
- 1½ cups unsweetened hemp milk
- ½ cup ice cubes

Instructions:

1. In a high-powered blender, put all ingredients and pulse until creamy and smooth.
2. Place the smoothie into four serving glasses and serve.

Nutritional Information per Serving:

Calories	: 318
Fat	: 16.1g
Saturated Fat	: 1.1g
Carbohydrates	: 43g
Fiber	: 5.5g
Sugar	: 31.4g
Protein	: 7.4g
Sodium	: 96mg

Strawberry Date Smoothie

Servings: 2

Preparation Time: 10 minutes

Ingredients:

- 1 cup fresh strawberries, hulled and sliced
- 2 Medjool dates, pitted and chopped
- 2 tablespoons almond butter
- 1 scoop unsweetened vegan vanilla protein powder
- 1½ cups unsweetened almond milk
- ¼ cup ice cubes

Instructions:

1. Add all the ingredients in a high-powered blender and pulse until creamy and smooth.
2. Pour the smoothie into two glasses and serve immediately.

Nutritional Information per Serving:

Calories	: 289
Fat	: 12.4g
Saturated Fat	: 0.9g
Carbohydrates	: 31g
Fiber	: 5.8g
Sugar	: 22.2g
Protein	: 18.3g
Sodium	: 269mg

Chapter 4: Plant-Based Smoothie & Juicing Recipes

Mocha Smoothie

 Servings: 2

 Preparation Time: 10 minutes

Ingredients:

- 1 large frozen banana, peeled and sliced
- 1 scoop unsweetened vegan protein powder
- 2 tablespoons cacao powder
- 1 cup cold brewed coffee
- 1 cup unsweetened almond milk

Instructions:

1. Add all the ingredients in a high-powered blender and pulse until creamy and smooth.
2. Pour the smoothie into two glasses and serve immediately.

Nutritional Information per Serving:

Calories	: 152
Fat	: 3.5g
Saturated Fat	: 0.9g
Carbohydrates	: 19g
Fiber	: 3.8g
Sugar	: 8.3g
Protein	: 15.1g
Sodium	: 225mg

Chocolaty Oats Smoothie

 Servings: 2

 Preparation Time: 10 minutes

Ingredients:

- 2 medium frozen bananas, peeled
- 4 dates, pitted
- 4 tablespoons peanut butter
- 4 tablespoons rolled oats
- 2 tablespoons cacao powder
- 2 tablespoons chia seeds
- 2 cups unsweetened soy milk

Instructions:

1. Add all the ingredients in a high-powered blender and pulse until creamy and smooth.
2. Pour the smoothie into two glasses and serve immediately.

Nutritional Information per Serving:

Calories	: 583
Fat	: 25.2g
Saturated Fat	: 4.8g
Carbohydrates	: 75g
Fiber	: 15.3g
Sugar	: 37.8g
Protein	: 23.1g
Sodium	: 200mg

Chapter 4: Plant-Based Smoothie & Juicing Recipes

Chocolaty Seeds Smoothie

Servings: 2

Preparation Time: 10 minutes

Ingredients:

- 2 large frozen bananas, peeled and sliced
- 2 tablespoons cacao powder
- 1 tablespoon hemp seeds
- 1 tablespoon chia seeds
- 1 tablespoon maca powder
- 1½ cups unsweetened coconut milk

Instructions:

1. Add all the ingredients in a high-powered blender and pulse until creamy and smooth.
2. Pour the smoothie into two glasses and serve immediately.

Nutritional Information per Serving:

Calories	: 449
Fat	: 29.2g
Saturated Fat	: 23.5g
Carbohydrates	: 41.3g
Fiber	: 6.9g
Sugar	: 21.6g
Protein	: 7.2g
Sodium	: 58mg

Chocolaty Strawberry Smoothie

Servings: 2

Preparation Time: 10 minutes

Ingredients:

- 2 cups fresh strawberries, hulled and sliced
- 1 large frozen banana, peeled and sliced
- 2 tablespoons cacao powder
- 1 teaspoon vanilla extract
- 1½ cups unsweetened almond milk

Instructions:

1. Add all the ingredients in a high-powered blender and pulse until creamy and smooth.
2. Pour the smoothie into two glasses and serve immediately.

Nutritional Information per Serving:

Calories	: 155
Fat	: 4.3g
Saturated Fat	: 0.9g
Carbohydrates	: 30.9g
Fiber	: 6.9g
Sugar	: 15.7g
Protein	: 3.5g
Sodium	: 137mg

Chapter 4: Plant-Based Smoothie & Juicing Recipes

Chocolaty Cherry Smoothie

Servings: 2

Preparation Time: 10 minutes

Ingredients:

- 2 cups fresh cherries, pitted
- 2 tablespoons cacao powder
- 2 teaspoons maple syrup
- ½ cup plain coconut yogurt
- 1½ cups unsweetened almond milk
- ¼ cup ice cubes

Instructions:

1. Add all the ingredients in a high-powered blender and pulse until creamy and smooth.
2. Pour the smoothie into two glasses and serve immediately.

Nutritional Information per Serving:

Calories	: 175
Fat	: 5.6g
Saturated Fat	: 2.6g
Carbohydrates	: 33.5g
Fiber	: 7.3g
Sugar	: 23.5g
Protein	: 3.8g
Sodium	: 183mg

Apple & Spinach Smoothie

Servings: 2

Preparation Time: 10 minutes

Ingredients:

- 2 medium apples, peeled, cored and chopped
- 1 banana, peeled and sliced
- 2 cups fresh spinach
- 1 scoop vegan protein powder
- 1 tablespoon hemp seeds
- 1 tablespoon chia seeds
- 1 cup coconut water
- ¾ cup ice cubes

Instructions:

1. Add all the ingredients in a high-powered blender and pulse until creamy and smooth.
2. Pour the smoothie into two glasses and serve immediately.

Nutritional Information per Serving:

Calories	: 292
Fat	: 4.8g
Saturated Fat	: 1g
Carbohydrates	: 53.4g
Fiber	: 10.3g
Sugar	: 34.1g
Protein	: 1.7g
Sodium	: 179mg

Low-Fat Smoothies

People dealing with high blood cholesterol levels and heart conditions cannot enjoy food with high-fat content. These low-fat smoothies provide a perfect fit for their low-fat diet. In these smoothies, there is a good use of fruits, veggies and plant-based dairy; therefore, there are no saturated fats present in these smoothies. Since these smoothies are low-fat, they do not contain bad cholesterol, which is responsible for elevating blood pressure and blood cholesterol levels.

Strawberry & Plum Smoothie

Servings: 2

Preparation Time: 10 minutes

Ingredients:

- 2 cups frozen strawberries
- 1 medium plum, pitted and chopped
- 1 cup brewed and cooled green tea
- 1½ cups unsweetened almond milk
- ¼ cup ice cubes

Instructions:

1. Add all the ingredients in a high-powered blender and pulse until creamy and smooth.
2. Pour the smoothie into two glasses and serve immediately.

Nutritional Information per Serving:

Calories	: 100
Fat	: 1g
Saturated Fat	: 0.1g
Carbohydrates	: 24g
Fiber	: 3.7g
Sugar	: 18.9g
Protein	: 0.5g
Sodium	: 55mg

Greens & Orange Smoothie

Servings: 2

Preparation Time: 10 minutes

Ingredients:

- 1 cup fresh spinach, chopped
- 1 cup fresh kale, chopped
- 2 oranges peeled, seeded and sectioned
- 1 frozen banana, peeled and sliced
- 1 tablespoon hemp seeds
- 1 cup ice cubes, crushed

Instructions:

1. Add all the ingredients in a high-powered blender and pulse until creamy and smooth.
2. Pour the smoothie into two glasses and serve immediately.

Nutritional Information per Serving:

Calories	: 108
Fat	: 0.3g
Saturated Fat	: 0.1g
Carbohydrates	: 26.4g
Fiber	: 4.4g
Sugar	: 14.8g
Protein	: 2.8g
Sodium	: 27mg

Chapter 4: Plant-Based Smoothie & Juicing Recipes

Kiwi & Cucumber Smoothie

 Servings: 2

Preparation Time: 10 minutes

Ingredients:

- 2 kiwi fruit, peeled and chopped
- 2 small cucumber, peeled and chopped
- 2 tablespoon fresh parsley leaves
- ½ teaspoon fresh ginger, peeled and chopped
- 2 cup chilled filtered water

Instructions:

1. Add all the ingredients in a high-powered blender and pulse until creamy and smooth.
2. Pour the smoothie into two glasses and serve immediately.

Nutritional Information per Serving:

Calories	: 94
Fat	: 0.8g
Saturated Fat	: 0.2g
Carbohydrates	: 22.6g
Fiber	: 4g
Sugar	: 11.9g
Protein	: 3g
Sodium	: 11mg

Raspberry, Cabbage & Tomato Smoothie

 Servings: 2

Preparation Time: 10 minutes

Ingredients:

- 1 cup fresh raspberries
- 1 cup red cabbage, chopped
- 1 small tomato, chopped
- 2 teaspoons maple syrup
- 2 cup chilled filtered water

Instructions:

1. Add all the ingredients in a high-powered blender and pulse until creamy and smooth.
2. Pour the smoothie into two glasses and serve immediately.

Nutritional Information per Serving:

Calories	: 70
Fat	: 0.5g
Saturated Fat	: 0g
Carbohydrates	: 16.9g
Fiber	: 5.4g
Sugar	: 10.8g
Protein	: 1.6g
Sodium	: 9mg

The Plant-Based Vegan: Juicing and Smoothie Diet Cookbook
200 Delicious Smoothie & Juicing Recipes To Lose Weight, Detox Your Body, and Live A Long Healthy Life

Chapter 4: Plant-Based Smoothie & Juicing Recipes

Melon & Cucumber Smoothie

 Servings: 2

 Preparation Time: 10 minutes

Ingredients:

- 2 cups dew melon, peeled and chopped
- 1 large cucumber, peeled and chopped
- 1 tablespoon fresh mint leaves
- 1 tablespoon maple syrup
- 2 tablespoons fresh lemon juice
- 1½ cups filtered water
- ¼ cup ice cubes

Instructions:

1. Add all the ingredients in a high-powered blender and pulse until creamy and smooth.
2. Pour the smoothie into two glasses and serve immediately.

Nutritional Information per Serving:

Calories	: 73
Fat	: 0.5g
Saturated Fat	: 0.2g
Carbohydrates	: 17.6g
Fiber	: 2g
Sugar	: 13.2g
Protein	: 1.9g
Sodium	: 30mg

Guava & Pineapple Smoothie

 Servings: 2

 Preparation Time: 10 minutes

Ingredients:

- 1 cup guava, seeds removed
- 1 large banana, peeled and sliced
- 1 cup pineapple chunks
- 1½ cup filtered water
- ½ cup ice cubes

Instructions:

1. Add all the ingredients in a high-powered blender and pulse until creamy and smooth.
2. Pour the smoothie into two glasses and serve immediately.

Nutritional Information per Serving:

Calories	: 150
Fat	: 1.1g
Saturated Fat	: 0.3g
Carbohydrates	: 36.1g
Fiber	: 7.1g
Sugar	: 22.7g
Protein	: 3.2g
Sodium	: 9mg

Chapter 4: Plant-Based Smoothie & Juicing Recipes

Apricot & Raspberry Smoothie

🛎 **Servings:** 2

🕐 **Preparation Time:**
10 minutes

Ingredients:

- 4 apricots, peeled and sliced
- 2/3 cup frozen raspberries
- 1 large banana, peeled and sliced
- 1½ cups water
- ¼ cup ice cubes

Instructions:

1. Add all the ingredients in a high-powered blender and pulse until creamy and smooth.
2. Pour the smoothie into two glasses and serve immediately.

Nutritional Information per Serving:

Calories	: 107
Fat	: 0.9g
Saturated Fat	: 0.1g
Carbohydrates	: 26.1g
Fiber	: 5.6g
Sugar	: 15.4g
Protein	: 2g
Sodium	: 15.4mg

Watermelon & Cucumber Smoothie

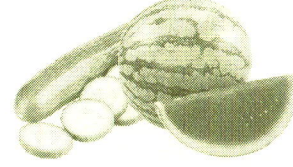

🛎 **Servings:** 2

🕐 **Preparation Time:**
10 minutes

Ingredients:

- 2 cups watermelon, cubed
- 2 small cucumbers, peeled and sliced
- ½ cup fresh mint leaves, chopped roughly
- 1-2 tablespoons maple syrup
- 1 tablespoon fresh lime juice
- 1 cup coconut water
- ½ cup ice cubes

Instructions:

1. Add all the ingredients in a high-powered blender and pulse until creamy and smooth.
2. Pour the smoothie into two glasses and serve immediately.

Nutritional Information per Serving:

Calories	: 140
Fat	: 1g
Saturated Fat	: 0.6g
Carbohydrates	: 32.2g
Fiber	: 5.6g
Sugar	: 19.1g
Protein	: 4.9g
Sodium	: 204mg

The Plant-Based Vegan: Juicing and Smoothie Diet Cookbook
200 Delicious Smoothie & Juicing Recipes To Lose Weight, Detox Your Body, and Live A Long Healthy Life

Chapter 4: Plant-Based Smoothie & Juicing Recipes

Coconut Green Smoothie

Servings: 2

Preparation Time: 10 minutes

Ingredients:

- 3 cups fresh spinach
- 1 (1-inch) piece fresh ginger, peeled
- ¼ cup unsweetened ground coconut
- ¼ teaspoon salt
- 1½ cup coconut water
- 1 cup ice

Instructions:

1. Add all the ingredients in a high-powered blender and pulse until creamy and smooth.
2. Pour the smoothie into two glasses and serve immediately.

Nutritional Information per Serving:

Calories	: 83
Fat	: 3g
Saturated Fat	: 2g
Carbohydrates	: 10.5g
Fiber	: 4g
Sugar	: 5.5g
Protein	: 3g
Sodium	: 518mg

Cranberry, Pear & Orange Smoothie

Servings: 2

Preparation Time: 10 minutes

Ingredients:

- ½ cup fresh cranberries
- 1 large pear, cored and chopped
- 1 (½-inch) piece fresh ginger, peeled
- 1 orange, peeled, seeded and sectioned
- 1 cup filtered water
- 1 cup ice cubes

Instructions:

1. Add all the ingredients in a high-powered blender and pulse until creamy and smooth.
2. Pour the smoothie into two glasses and serve immediately.

Nutritional Information per Serving:

Calories	: 94
Fat	: 0.2g
Saturated Fat	: 0g
Carbohydrates	: 23.2g
Fiber	: 5g
Sugar	: 16.1g
Protein	: 1.1g
Sodium	: 1mg

Protein-Packed Smoothies

The plant-based diet is often termed a low-protein diet, which is why most people avoid having it. However, with selecting the right kind of protein-packed ingredients, it is possible to increase your daily protein intake. These smoothies are created with the sole purpose to increase the protein content of your plant-based diet. They are prepared using a mix of various vegan protein powder with fruits, veggies and liquid bases.

Chapter 4: Plant-Based Smoothie & Juicing Recipes

Peanut Butter Smoothie

Servings: 2

Preparation Time: 10 minutes

Ingredients:

- 2 medium frozen bananas, peeled and sliced
- 2 scoops unsweetened vegan protein powder
- 3 tablespoons natural peanut butter
- 2 tablespoons nutritional yeast
- 1½ cups unsweetened almond milk

Instructions:

1. Add all the ingredients in a high-powered blender and pulse until creamy and smooth.
2. Pour the smoothie into two glasses and serve immediately.

Nutritional Information per Serving:

Calories	: 425
Fat	: 16.5g
Saturated Fat	: 2.7g
Carbohydrates	: 42.3g
Fiber	: 7.8g
Sugar	: 17.8g
Protein	: 33.1g
Sodium	: 280mg

Vanilla Smoothie

Servings: 2

Preparation Time: 10 minutes

Ingredients:

- ½ cup unsweetened vegan vanilla protein powder
- 4 tablespoons almond butter
- 2 teaspoons vanilla extract
- 6-8 drops liquid stevia
- 2 cups unsweetened almond milk
- ¼ cup ice cubes

Instructions:

1. Add all the ingredients in a high-powered blender and pulse until creamy and smooth.
2. Pour the smoothie into two glasses and serve immediately.

Nutritional Information per Serving:

Calories	: 355
Fat	: 22.7g
Saturated Fat	: 2g
Carbohydrates	: 10.4g
Fiber	: 4.2g
Sugar	: 3.2g
Protein	: 29.8g
Sodium	: 231mg

Chapter 4: Plant-Based Smoothie & Juicing Recipes

Apple Smoothie

 Servings: 2

Preparation Time: 10 minutes

Ingredients:

- 1 ounce rolled oats
- 2 apples, peeled, cored and chopped roughly
- 2 scoops unsweetened vegan protein powder
- 2 tablespoons chia seeds
- 1 teaspoon stevia powder
- ½ teaspoon ground cinnamon
- 8 ounces coconut yogurt
- 1 cup unsweetened almond milk
- ½ cup ice cubes

Instructions:

1. Add all the ingredients in a high-powered blender and pulse until creamy and smooth.
2. Pour the smoothie into two glasses and serve immediately.

Nutritional Information per Serving:

Calories	: 492
Fat	: 13.2g
Saturated Fat	: 4.7g
Carbohydrates	: 69.2g
Fiber	: 11g
Sugar	: 42.5g
Protein	: 30.4g
Sodium	: 316mg

Raspberry Smoothie

 Servings: 2

Preparation Time: 10 minutes

Ingredients:

- 1¼ cups fresh raspberries
- 2 bananas, peeled and sliced
- ½ cup oats
- 1 scoop unsweetened vegan protein powder
- 1 tablespoon maple syrup
- 1 tablespoon chia seeds
- 1½ cups unsweetened almond milk
- ¼ cup ice cubes

Instructions:

1. Add all the ingredients in a high-powered blender and pulse until creamy and smooth.
2. Pour the smoothie into two glasses and serve immediately.

Nutritional Information per Serving:

Calories	: 345
Fat	: 6.6g
Saturated Fat	: 0.7g
Carbohydrates	: 62.1g
Fiber	: 12.1g
Sugar	: 24.9g
Protein	: 15.9g
Sodium	: 206mg

Chapter 4: Plant-Based Smoothie & Juicing Recipes

Mango Tofu Smoothie

Servings: 2

Preparation Time: 10 minutes

Ingredients:

- 2 medium frozen bananas, peeled and sliced
- 2 scoops unsweetened vegan protein powder
- 3 tablespoons natural peanut butter
- 2 tablespoons nutritional yeast
- 1½ cups unsweetened almond milk

Instructions:

1. Add all the ingredients in a high-powered blender and pulse until creamy and smooth.
2. Pour the smoothie into two glasses and serve immediately.

Nutritional Information per Serving:

Calories	: 282
Fat	: 6.5g
Saturated Fat	: 0g
Carbohydrates	: 48g
Fiber	: 5.3g
Sugar	: 34.7g
Protein	: 13.1g
Sodium	: 75mg

Strawberry Smoothie

Servings: 2

Preparation Time: 10 minutes

Ingredients:

- 1½ cups fresh strawberries, hulled
- 1 large frozen banana, peeled
- 2 scoops unsweetened vegan vanilla protein powder
- 2 tablespoons hemp seeds
- 2 cups unsweetened hemp milk

Instructions:

1. In a high-speed blender, place all the ingredients and pulse until creamy and smooth.
2. Pour into two glasses and serve immediately.

Nutritional Information per Serving:

Calories	: 325
Fat	: 13g
Saturated Fat	: 0.8g
Carbohydrates	: 23.3g
Fiber	: 3.9g
Sugar	: 12.5g
Protein	: 31.2g
Sodium	: 391mg

Maca Smoothie

Servings: 2

Preparation Time: 10 minutes

Ingredients:

- 2 large frozen bananas, peeled and sliced
- 4 tablespoons sunflower seeds
- 2 tablespoon sunflower butter
- 1 scoop unsweetened vegan protein powder
- 1 tablespoon maca powder
- 1 teaspoon ground cinnamon
- ½ teaspoon pure vanilla extract
- 1½ cups unsweetened soy milk

Instructions:

1. Add all the ingredients in a high-powered blender and pulse until creamy and smooth.
2. Pour the smoothie into two glasses and serve immediately.

Nutritional Information per Serving:

Calories	: 404
Fat	: 14.8g
Saturated Fat	: 1.6g
Carbohydrates	: 46.6g
Fiber	: 5.8g
Sugar	: 22.6g
Protein	: 24.9g
Sodium	: 228mg

Kiwi Smoothie

Servings: 2

Preparation Time: 10 minutes

Ingredients:

- 3 kiwi fruits, peeled
- 2 bananas, peeled and sliced
- 4 tablespoons oats
- ½ teaspoon fresh ginger, peeled and chopped
- 1 teaspoon maple syrup
- 1 scoop unsweetened vegan protein powder
- ¾ cup coconut yogurt
- 1¼ cups unsweetened soy milk

Instructions:

1. Add all the ingredients in a high-powered blender and pulse until creamy and smooth.
2. Pour the smoothie into two glasses and serve immediately.

Nutritional Information per Serving:

Calories	: 3428
Fat	: 9g
Saturated Fat	: 4.3g
Carbohydrates	: 66.9g
Fiber	: 8.5g
Sugar	: 35.9g
Protein	: 26.2g
Sodium	: 238mg

Chapter 4: Plant-Based Smoothie & Juicing Recipes

Fruity Tofu Smoothie

Servings: 2
Preparation Time: 10 minutes

Ingredients:

- 12 ounces silken tofu, pressed and drained
- 2 medium bananas, peeled
- 1½ cups fresh blueberries
- 1 tablespoon maple syrup
- 1½ cups unsweetened soy milk
- ¼ cup ice cubes

Instructions:

1. Add all the ingredients in a high-powered blender and pulse until creamy and smooth.
2. Pour the smoothie into two glasses and serve immediately.

Nutritional Information per Serving:

Calories	: 398
Fat	: 8.6g
Saturated Fat	: 1.2g
Carbohydrates	: 65g
Fiber	: 7g
Sugar	: 50.7g
Protein	: 19.9g
Sodium	: 58mg

Pumpkin Smoothie

Servings: 2
Preparation Time: 10 minutes

Ingredients:

- ½ cup canned pumpkin
- 2 scoops unsweetened vegan protein powder
- ¼-½ teaspoon stevia powder
- ¼ teaspoon pumpkin pie spice
- ½ teaspoon vanilla extract
- 1½ cups unsweetened almond milk
- ½ cup ice cubes

Instructions:

1. Add all the ingredients in a high-powered blender and pulse until creamy and smooth.
2. Pour the smoothie into four glasses and serve immediately.

Nutritional Information per Serving:

Calories	: 171
Fat	: 3.9g
Saturated Fat	: 0.3g
Carbohydrates	: 6.7g
Fiber	: 2.6g
Sugar	: 2.2g
Protein	: 26.8g
Sodium	: 402mg

Chapter 4: Plant-Based Smoothie & Juicing Recipes

PB&J Smoothie

Servings: 2

Preparation Time: 10 minutes

Ingredients:

- 1 cup unsweetened almond milk
- ½ cup frozen strawberries
- 1 tbsp peanut butter
- 1 scoop vanilla protein powder

Instructions:

1. Add all the ingredients in a high-powered blender and pulse until creamy and smooth.
2. Pour the smoothie into four glasses and serve immediately.

Nutritional Information per Serving:

Calories	: 156
Fat	: 11g
Saturated Fat	: 2g
Carbohydrates	: 10g
Fiber	: 3g
Sugar	: 2.2g
Protein	: 6g
Sodium	: 402mg

Healthy Protein Coffee Smoothie

Servings: 2

Preparation Time: 10 minutes

Ingredients:

- ¾ cup dairy-free milk
- 1 cup fresh spinach
- 3 dates
- 1 scoop plant-based protein
- 2 tbsp cacao powder
- 2 tsp chia seeds
- ½ tsp finely ground espresso
- ¼ tsp vanilla bean powder
- ¼ tsp cinnamon
- ¼ tsp sea salt
- Ice cubes

Instructions:

1. Add all the ingredients in a high-powered blender and pulse until creamy and smooth.
2. Pour the smoothie into four glasses and serve immediately.

Nutritional Information per Serving:

Calories	: 238
Fat	: 8g
Saturated Fat	: 1g
Carbohydrates	: 28g
Fiber	: 10g
Sugar	: 14g
Protein	: 21g
Sodium	: 674mg

Weight-Loss Smoothies

Weight loss is possible when you increase your metabolic rates and reduce the caloric intake to where there are no excess calories for your body to store in the form of fat. These smoothies can be incorporated into your diet to achieve weight loss! What makes them so effective? Well, these smoothies have metabolic boosters and fat burners that allow the body to burn more calories and stored fats. Not only this, but these smoothies also contain low-carb, low-fat and low-caloric content, which helps in weight management.

Cherry Smoothie

Servings: 2

Preparation Time: 10 minutes

Ingredients:

- 1½ cups fresh cherries
- Pinch of ground cinnamon
- 3-4 drops liquid stevia
- 1½ cups unsweetened almond milk
- ½ cup ice cubes

Instructions:

1. Add all the ingredients in a high-powered blender and pulse until creamy and smooth.
2. Pour the smoothie into two glasses and serve immediately.

Nutritional Information per Serving:

Calories	: 80
Fat	: 2.6g
Saturated Fat	: 0.2g
Carbohydrates	: 14g
Fiber	: 2.3g
Sugar	: 9.5g
Protein	: 1.8g
Sodium	: 135mg

Carrot, Tomato & Celery Smoothie

Servings: 2

Preparation Time: 10 minutes

Ingredients:

- 4 medium tomatoes
- 1 large carrot, peeled and chopped
- 1 celery stalk, chopped
- Pinch of salt
- ¼ teaspoon ground black pepper
- 2 teaspoons fresh lemon juice
- 1 cup ice cubes

Instructions:

1. Add all the ingredients in a high-powered blender and pulse until creamy and smooth.
2. Pour the smoothie into two glasses and serve immediately.

Nutritional Information per Serving:

Calories	: 62
Fat	: 0.6g
Saturated Fat	: 0.1g
Carbohydrates	: 13.6g
Fiber	: 4.1g
Sugar	: 8.5g
Protein	: 2.6g
Sodium	: 122mg

Chapter 4: Plant-Based Smoothie & Juicing Recipes

Peach & Mango Smoothie

Servings: 2
Preparation Time: 10 minutes

Ingredients:

- 1 cup frozen peaches, pitted and chopped
- ½ cup frozen mango, peeled, pitted and cubed
- 1 teaspoon maple syrup
- 1½ cups unsweetened almond milk

Instructions:

1. Add all the ingredients in a high-powered blender and pulse until creamy and smooth.
2. Pour the smoothie into two glasses and serve immediately.

Nutritional Information per Serving:

Calories	: 93
Fat	: 3g
Saturated Fat	: 0.3g
Carbohydrates	: 16.9g
Fiber	: 2.6g
Sugar	: 14.6g
Protein	: 1.8g
Sodium	: 136mg

Strawberry & Orange Smoothie

Servings: 2
Preparation Time: 10 minutes

Ingredients:

- 1 cup frozen strawberries
- 1 frozen banana, peeled and sliced
- 1 cup unsweetened almond milk
- ½ cup fresh orange juice

Instructions:

1. Add all the ingredients in a high-powered blender and pulse until creamy and smooth.
2. Pour the smoothie into two glasses and serve immediately.

Nutritional Information per Serving:

Calories	: 124
Fat	: 2.3g
Saturated Fat	: 0.2g
Carbohydrates	: 26.5g
Fiber	: 3.6g
Sugar	: 16g
Protein	: 2g
Sodium	: 92mg

Chapter 4: Plant-Based Smoothie & Juicing Recipes

Melon Smoothie

Servings: 2

Preparation Time: 10 minutes

Ingredients:

- 2 cups honeydew melon, peeled, seeded and chopped
- 1 banana, peeled and sliced
- 1½ cups unsweetened almond milk
- ¼ cup ice cubes

Instructions:

1. Add all the ingredients in a high-powered blender and pulse until creamy and smooth.
2. Pour the smoothie into two glasses and serve immediately.

Nutritional Information per Serving:

Calories	: 111
Fat	: 2.8g
Saturated Fat	: 0.3g
Carbohydrates	: 22g
Fiber	: 2.3g
Sugar	: 7.2g
Protein	: 1.4g
Sodium	: 144mg

Melon & Mango Smoothie

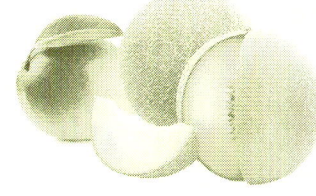

Servings: 2

Preparation Time: 10 minutes

Ingredients:

- 1 cup melon, peeled, seeded and chopped
- 1 cup mango, peeled, pitted and chopped
- 1 (½-inch) piece fresh ginger, peeled
- 1½ cups unsweetened almond milk

Instructions:

1. Add all the ingredients in a high-powered blender and pulse until creamy and smooth.
2. Pour the smoothie into two glasses and serve immediately.

Nutritional Information per Serving:

Calories	: 106
Fat	: 3.1g
Saturated Fat	: 0.4g
Carbohydrates	: 20.3g
Fiber	: 2.8g
Sugar	: 17.4g
Protein	: 2.1g
Sodium	: 148mg

Chapter 4: Plant-Based Smoothie & Juicing Recipes

Pear, Grapes & Kale Smoothie

Servings: 2
Preparation Time: 10 minutes

Ingredients:

- 1 pear, peeled, cored and chopped
- 1 cup seedless green grapes
- 2 cup fresh kale, chopped
- 3-4 drops liquid stevia
- 1 tablespoon fresh lime juice
- 1½ cups filtered water
- ½ cup ice cubes

Instructions:

1. Add all the ingredients in a high-powered blender and pulse until creamy and smooth.
2. Pour the smoothie into two glasses and serve immediately.

Nutritional Information per Serving:

Calories	: 132
Fat	: 0.1g
Saturated Fat	: 0g
Carbohydrates	: 32.7g
Fiber	: 3.7g
Sugar	: 19.6g
Protein	: 2.3g
Sodium	: 32mg

Apple, Pear & Avocado Smoothie

Servings: 2
Preparation Time: 10 minutes

Ingredients:

- 1 green apple, peeled, cored and sliced
- 1 pear, peeled, cored and sliced
- 1 small avocado, peeled, pitted and chopped
- 1 cup fresh baby kale
- 3-4 drops liquid stevia
- 1 cup coconut water
- 1 cup ice cubes

Instructions:

1. Add all the ingredients in a high-powered blender and pulse until creamy and smooth.
2. Pour the smoothie into two glasses and serve immediately.

Nutritional Information per Serving:

Calories	: 150
Fat	: 5g
Saturated Fat	: 2g
Carbohydrates	: 25g
Fiber	: 7g
Sugar	: 14.3g
Protein	: 2.9g
Sodium	: 137mg

The Plant-Based Vegan: Juicing and Smoothie Diet Cookbook
200 Delicious Smoothie & Juicing Recipes To Lose Weight, Detox Your Body, and Live A Long Healthy Life

Chapter 4: Plant-Based Smoothie & Juicing Recipes

Spinach, Strawberry & Orange Smoothie

Servings: 2

Preparation Time: 10 minutes

Ingredients:

- 1 cup frozen strawberries
- 2 cups fresh spinach
- 1 cup fresh orange juice
- 1 cup water

Instructions:

1. Add all the ingredients in a high-powered blender and pulse until creamy and smooth.
2. Pour the smoothie into two glasses and serve immediately.

Nutritional Information per Serving:

Calories	: 86
Fat	: 0.6g
Saturated Fat	: 0.1g
Carbohydrates	: 19.5g
Fiber	: 2.4g
Sugar	: 14.1g
Protein	: 2.2g
Sodium	: 25mg

Apple, Cucumber & Spinach Smoothie

Servings: 2

Preparation Time: 10 minutes

Ingredients:

- 2 green apples, peeled, cored and chopped
- 2 cups fresh baby spinach
- 1 small cucumber, peeled and chopped
- 1½ cups filtered water
- ¼ cup ice cubes

Instructions:

1. Add all the ingredients in a high-powered blender and pulse until creamy and smooth.
2. Pour the smoothie into two glasses and serve immediately.

Nutritional Information per Serving:

Calories	: 145
Fat	: 0.7g
Saturated Fat	: 0.1g
Carbohydrates	: 37.4g
Fiber	: 6.8g
Sugar	: 25.8g
Protein	: 2.4g
Sodium	: 29mg

CHAPTER 05

Plant-Based Juicing Recipes

Brain Healthy Juices

The human brain takes a large chunk of energy produced in the body through the consumption of food. For this reason, having nutritious, loaded, and energizing food on the menu can help boost brain functioning. The brain nourishing juices are prepared in such a way that they could provide all the super nutritious and cell-rejuvenating ingredients in a single glass. These juices are especially healthy for growing kids, people having loss of concentration and focus, and those suffering from a variety of brain disorders.

Chapter 5: Plant-Based Juicing Recipes

Blueberry Juice

Servings: 2

Preparation Time: 10 minutes

Ingredients:

- 4 cups fresh blueberries
- 1-2 teaspoons cane sugar
- 1 tablespoon fresh lime juice

Instructions:

1. Add all the ingredients in a juicer and extract the juice according to the manufacturer's method.
2. Pour into two glasses and serve immediately.

Nutritional Information per Serving:

Calories	: 174
Fat	: 1g
Saturated Fat	: 0g
Carbohydrates	: 44.1g
Fiber	: 7g
Sugar	: 30.8g
Protein	: 2.2g
Sodium	: 2mg

Strawberry & Apple Juice

Servings: 2

Preparation Time: 10 minutes

Ingredients:

- 2½ cups fresh ripe strawberries, hulled
- 1 large apple, cored and chopped roughly
- 1 lemon, peeled

Instructions:

1. Add all the ingredients in a juicer and extract the juice according to the manufacturer's method.
2. Pour into two glasses and serve immediately.

Nutritional Information per Serving:

Calories	: 118
Fat	: 0.8g
Saturated Fat	: 0g
Carbohydrates	: 30.1g
Fiber	: 6.5g
Sugar	: 20.6g
Protein	: 1.6g
Sodium	: 3mg

Chapter 5: Plant-Based Juicing Recipes

Berries & Carrot Juice

⌂ **Servings:** 2

⏱ **Preparation Time:**
10 minutes

Ingredients:

- 1 cup fresh strawberries
- 1 fresh cups blueberries
- 1 cup fresh raspberries
- 6 medium carrots

Instructions:

1. Add all the ingredients in a juicer and extract the juice according to the manufacturer's method.
2. Pour into two glasses and serve immediately.

Nutritional Information per Serving:

Calories	: 172
Fat	: 0.9g
Saturated Fat	: 0g
Carbohydrates	: 41.4g
Fiber	: 11.7g
Sugar	: 22.5g
Protein	: 3.3g
Sodium	: 128mg

Cranberry, Apple & Orange Juice

⌂ **Servings:** 2

⏱ **Preparation Time:**
10 minutes

Ingredients:

- 1 cup fresh cranberries
- 3 apples, cored and sliced
- 1 sweet potato, peeled and quartered
- 3 large carrots
- 2 oranges, peeled and sectioned

Instructions:

1. Add all the ingredients in a juicer and extract the juice according to the manufacturer's method.
2. Pour into two glasses and serve immediately.

Nutritional Information per Serving:

Calories	: 398
Fat	: 0.9g
Saturated Fat	: 0g
Carbohydrates	: 97.9g
Fiber	: 19.5g
Sugar	: 63.9g
Protein	: 4.9g
Sodium	: 103mg

The Plant-Based Vegan: Juicing and Smoothie Diet Cookbook
200 Delicious Smoothie & Juicing Recipes To Lose Weight, Detox Your Body, and Live A Long Healthy Life

Chapter 5: Plant-Based Juicing Recipes

Carrot Juice

 Servings: 2

 Preparation Time: 10 minutes

Ingredients:

- 4 large carrots, peeled and chopped roughly
- ½ lemon, peeled and chopped roughly
- ½ inch fresh ginger, peeled
- 1½ cups filtered water

Instructions:

1. Add all the ingredients in a juicer and extract the juice according to the manufacturer's method.
2. Pour into two glasses and serve immediately.

Nutritional Information per Serving:

Calories	: 68
Fat	: 0.2g
Saturated Fat	: 0g
Carbohydrates	: 16.4g
Fiber	: 4g
Sugar	: 7.3g
Protein	: 1.5g
Sodium	: 100mg

Carrot, Beet & Spinach Juice

 Servings: 2

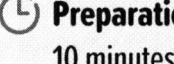 **Preparation Time:** 10 minutes

Ingredients:

- 4 cups carrot, peeled and chopped roughly
- 2 cups beet, trimmed and peeled
- 3 cups fresh spinach

Instructions:

1. Add all the ingredients in a juicer and extract the juice according to the manufacturer's method.
2. Pour into two glasses and serve immediately.

Nutritional Information per Serving:

Calories	: 175
Fat	: 0.5g
Saturated Fat	: 0.1g
Carbohydrates	: 40.2g
Fiber	: 9.8g
Sugar	: 24.5g
Protein	: 6g
Sodium	: 318mg

The Plant-Based Vegan: Juicing and Smoothie Diet Cookbook
200 Delicious Smoothie & Juicing Recipes To Lose Weight, Detox Your Body, and Live A Long Healthy Life

Chapter 5: Plant-Based Juicing Recipes

Matcha Green Juice

Ingredients:

- 6 ounces fresh kale
- ¼ cup fresh parsley
- 4 celery stalks
- 2 large apples, cored and chopped roughly
- 1 (1-inch) piece fresh ginger, peeled
- 1 lemon, peeled
- ½ teaspoon matcha green tea

Instructions:

1. Add all the ingredients in a juicer and extract the juice according to the manufacturer's method.
2. Pour into 2 glasses and serve immediately.

Servings: 2

Preparation Time: 10 minutes

Nutritional Information per Serving:

Calories	: 113
Fat	: 0.6g
Saturated Fat	: 0.1g
Carbohydrates	: 26.7g
Fiber	: 5.2g
Sugar	: 12.9g
Protein	: 3.8g
Sodium	: 71mg

Kale, Carrot & Grapefruit Juice

Ingredients:

- 3 cups fresh kale
- 2 large green apples, cored and sliced
- 2 medium carrots, peeled and chopped roughly
- 2 medium grapefruit, peeled and sectioned
- 1 teaspoon fresh lemon juice

Instructions:

1. Add all the ingredients in a juicer and extract the juice according to the manufacturer's method.
2. Pour into 2 glasses and serve immediately.

Servings: 2

Preparation Time: 10 minutes

Nutritional Information per Serving:

Calories	: 332
Fat	: 0.6g
Saturated Fat	: 0g
Carbohydrates	: 57.7g
Fiber	: 9.8g
Sugar	: 35.2g
Protein	: 4.9g
Sodium	: 88mg

Chapter 5: Plant-Based Juicing Recipes

Apple, Kale & Cucumber Juice

Servings: 2

Preparation Time: 10 minutes

Ingredients:

- 4 cups fresh kale
- 2 cucumbers, chopped roughly
- 2 large granny smith apples, cored and sliced
- 1 large lemon peeled and quartered

Instructions:

1. Add all the ingredients in a juicer and extract the juice according to the manufacturer's method.
2. Pour into two glasses and serve immediately.

Nutritional Information per Serving:

Calories	: 229
Fat	: 0.8g
Saturated Fat	: 0.1g
Carbohydrates	: 56.5g
Fiber	: 9.1g
Sugar	: 28.4g
Protein	: 6.7g
Sodium	: 66mg

Citrus & Ginger Green Juice

Servings: 2

Preparation Time: 10 minutes

Ingredients:

- 3 cups fresh Swiss chard
- 4 celery stalks
- 2 cucumber, chopped roughly
- 1 bunch fresh cilantro
- 1 lime
- 1 (2-inch) piece fresh ginger, peeled

Instructions:

1. Add all the ingredients in a juicer and extract the juice according to the manufacturer's method.
2. Pour into two glasses and serve immediately.

Nutritional Information per Serving:

Calories	: 82
Fat	: 0.9g
Saturated Fat	: 0.2g
Carbohydrates	: 18.6g
Fiber	: 3.9g
Sugar	: 6.4g
Protein	: 3.7g
Sodium	: 151mg

Cleansing & Detoxifying Juices

Juices that are cleansing and detoxifying are bliss for the mind and the body. These juices are prepared using leafy greens and items like green tea, lime and lemon juices which enrich them with more radical scavengers- the antioxidants. These juices have the extracts of a variety of vegetables and fruits, which together create this cleansing effect.

Chapter 5: Plant-Based Juicing Recipes

Orange Juice

🍽 **Servings:** 2

🕐 **Preparation Time:** 10 minutes

Nutritional Information per Serving:

Calories	: 346
Fat	: 0.9g
Saturated Fat	: 0.1g
Carbohydrates	: 86.5g
Fiber	: 13.3g
Sugar	: 68.8g
Protein	: 6.9g
Sodium	: 0mg

Ingredients:

- 8 large oranges, peeled and sectioned

Instructions:

1. Add all the ingredients in a juicer and extract the juice according to the manufacturer's method.
2. Pour into two glasses and serve immediately.

Orange & Carrot Juice

🍽 **Servings:** 2

🕐 **Preparation Time:** 10 minutes

Nutritional Information per Serving:

Calories	: 311
Fat	: 0.7g
Saturated Fat	: 0.1g
Carbohydrates	: 77.2g
Fiber	: 16.3g
Sugar	: 57.7g
Protein	: 6.2g
Sodium	: 84mg

Ingredients:

- 6 medium oranges, peeled and sectioned
- 4 carrots, peeled and chopped roughly
- 1 (2-inch) piece fresh ginger, peeled

Instructions:

1. Add all the ingredients in a juicer and extract the juice according to the manufacturer's method.
2. Pour into two glasses and serve immediately.

The Plant-Based Vegan: Juicing and Smoothie Diet Cookbook
200 Delicious Smoothie & Juicing Recipes To Lose Weight, Detox Your Body, and Live A Long Healthy Life

Chapter 5: Plant-Based Juicing Recipes

Grapefruit, Apple & Carrot Juice

Servings: 2

Preparation Time: 10 minutes

Ingredients:

- 2 large Granny Smith apples, cored and sliced
- 4 medium carrots, peeled and chopped roughly
- 2 large grapefruit, peeled and seeded
- 1 teaspoon fresh lemon juice

Instructions:

1. Add all the ingredients in a juicer and extract the juice according to the manufacturer's method.
2. Pour into two glasses and serve immediately.

Nutritional Information per Serving:

Calories	: 208
Fat	: 0.6g
Saturated Fat	: 0g
Carbohydrates	: 53.2g
Fiber	: 9.8g
Sugar	: 38.2g
Protein	: 2.4g
Sodium	: 87mg

Apple Juice

Servings: 2

Preparation Time: 10 minutes

Ingredients:

- 6 large apples, cored and chopped roughly
- 1 small lemon

Instructions:

1. Add all the ingredients in a juicer and extract the juice according to the manufacturer's method.
2. Pour into two glasses and serve immediately.

Nutritional Information per Serving:

Calories	: 350
Fat	: 1.2g
Saturated Fat	: 0g
Carbohydrates	: 93.1g
Fiber	: 16.4g
Sugar	: 69.8g
Protein	: 1.9g
Sodium	: 0mg

Chapter 5: Plant-Based Juicing Recipes

Apple & Carrot Juice

Servings: 2

Preparation Time: 10 minutes

Ingredients:

- 5 carrots, peeled and chopped roughly
- 2 large apple, cored and chopped roughly
- 1 (½-inch) piece fresh ginger, peeled and chopped roughly
- ½ of lemon

Instructions:

1. Add all the ingredients in a juicer and extract the juice according to the manufacturer's method.
2. Pour into two glasses and serve immediately.

Nutritional Information per Serving:

Calories	: 135
Fat	: 0.3g
Saturated Fat	: 0g
Carbohydrates	: 33g
Fiber	: 7g
Sugar	: 21g
Protein	: 1.8g
Sodium	: 106mg

Apple & Pomegranate Juice

Servings: 2

Preparation Time: 10 minutes

Ingredients:

- 2 cups fresh pomegranate seeds
- 2 large Granny Smith apples, cored and sliced
- 2 teaspoons fresh lemon juice
- Pinch of freshly ground black pepper

Instructions:

1. Add all the ingredients in a juicer and extract the juice according to the manufacturer's method.
2. Pour into two glasses and serve immediately.

Nutritional Information per Serving:

Calories	: 242
Fat	: 0.4g
Saturated Fat	: 0g
Carbohydrates	: 60.9g
Fiber	: 6.7g
Sugar	: 37.3g
Protein	: 1.8g
Sodium	: 3mg

The Plant-Based Vegan: Juicing and Smoothie Diet Cookbook
200 Delicious Smoothie & Juicing Recipes To Lose Weight, Detox Your Body, and Live A Long Healthy Life

Chapter 5: Plant-Based Juicing Recipes

Apple, Orange & Broccoli Juice

Servings: 2

Preparation Time: 10 minutes

Ingredients:

- 2 broccoli stalks, chopped roughly
- 2 large green apples, cored and sliced
- 3 large oranges, peeled and sectioned
- 4 tablespoons fresh parsley

Instructions:

1. Add all the ingredients in a juicer and extract the juice according to the manufacturer's method.
2. Pour into two glasses and serve immediately.

Nutritional Information per Serving:

Calories	: 254
Fat	: 0.8g
Saturated Fat	: 0.1g
Carbohydrates	: 64.7g
Fiber	: 12.7g
Sugar	: 49.3g
Protein	: 3.8g
Sodium	: 11mg

Red Fruit & Veggies Juice

Servings: 2

Preparation Time: 10 minutes

Ingredients:

- 2 beets, peeled and roughly diced
- 1 large red bell pepper, seeded and chopped roughly
- 1 large tomato, seeded and chopped roughly
- 2 large red apples, cored and sliced
- 2½ cups fresh strawberries, hulled and sliced
- ¼ cup fresh mint leaves

Instructions:

1. Add all the ingredients in a juicer and extract the juice according to the manufacturer's method.
2. Transfer into two glasses and serve immediately.

Nutritional Information per Serving:

Calories	: 258
Fat	: 1.5g
Saturated Fat	: 0.1g
Carbohydrates	: 63.6g
Fiber	: 13.7g
Sugar	: 45.4g
Protein	: 5.3g
Sodium	: 90mg

Chapter 5: Plant-Based Juicing Recipes

Celery, Carrot & Orange Juice

Servings: 2
Preparation Time: 10 minutes

Ingredients:

- 4 celery stalks with leaves
- 3 medium carrots, peeled and chopped roughly
- 2 oranges, peeled and sectioned
- 1 tablespoon fresh ginger, peeled

Instructions:

1. Add all the ingredients in a juicer and extract the juice according to the manufacturer's method.
2. Pour into two glasses and serve immediately.

Nutritional Information per Serving:

Calories	: 139
Fat	: 0.4g
Saturated Fat	: 0.1g
Carbohydrates	: 33.5g
Fiber	: 7.6g
Sugar	: 22.3g
Protein	: 3g
Sodium	: 91mg

Cucumber, Apple & Carrot Juice

Servings: 2
Preparation Time: 10 minutes

Ingredients:

- 5 carrots, peeled and chopped roughly
- 1 large apple, cored and chopped roughly
- 1 large cucumber, chopped roughly
- 1 (½-inch) piece fresh ginger, peeled and chopped roughly
- ½ of lemon

Instructions:

1. Add all the ingredients in a juicer and extract the juice according to the manufacturer's method.
2. Pour into two glasses and serve immediately.

Nutritional Information per Serving:

Calories	: 154
Fat	: 0.5g
Saturated Fat	: 0.1g
Carbohydrates	: 38.1g
Fiber	: 7.7g
Sugar	: 21.8g
Protein	: 2.8g
Sodium	: 110mg

Digestive Health Juices

Our digestive system has various organs and glands working in harmony to make digestion and absorption of nutrients possible. Inside our gut system, there are friendly bacteria that aids in digestion. Food used in these juices supports the gut biome and improves internal gut health by providing necessary probiotics. Other nutrients present in these juices can speed up the digestion process by managing the release of enzymes and hormones.

Chapter 5: Plant-Based Juicing Recipes

Watermelon Juice

Servings: 2

Preparation Time: 10 minutes

Ingredients:

- 4 cups fresh watermelon, seeded and chopped roughly
- Pinch of salt
- Pinch of freshly ground black pepper

Instructions:

1. Add all the ingredients in a juicer and extract the juice according to the manufacturer's method.
2. Pour into two glasses and serve immediately.

Nutritional Information per Serving:

Calories	: 91
Fat	: 0.4g
Saturated Fat	: 0.2g
Carbohydrates	: 22.9g
Fiber	: 1.2g
Sugar	: 18.7g
Protein	: 1.8g
Sodium	: 82mg

Pomegranate Juice

Servings: 2

Preparation Time: 10 minutes

Ingredients:

- 2 cups pomegranate seeds
- 2 teaspoons coconut sugar
- Pinch of salt
- 1 cup filtered water

Instructions:

1. Add all the ingredients in a juicer and extract the juice according to the manufacturer's method.
2. Pour into two glasses and serve immediately.

Nutritional Information per Serving:

Calories	: 265
Fat	: 0g
Saturated Fat	: 0g
Carbohydrates	: 64g
Fiber	: 2.5g
Sugar	: 3.4g
Protein	: 2.5g
Sodium	: 78mg

The Plant-Based Vegan: Juicing and Smoothie Diet Cookbook
200 Delicious Smoothie & Juicing Recipes To Lose Weight, Detox Your Body, and Live A Long Healthy Life

Chapter 5: Plant-Based Juicing Recipes

Pineapple, Orange & Carrot Juice

 Servings: 2

 Preparation Time: 10 minutes

Ingredients:

- ½ pineapple, peeled and chopped roughly
- 4 oranges, peeled and sectioned
- 2 large carrots, peeled and chopped roughly
- 1 lemon, halved

Instructions:

1. Add all the ingredients in a juicer and extract the juice according to the manufacturer's method.
2. Pour into two glasses and serve immediately.

Nutritional Information per Serving:

Calories	: 312
Fat	: 0.7g
Saturated Fat	: 0.1g
Carbohydrates	: 79.5g
Fiber	: 13.7g
Sugar	: 59.8g
Protein	: 5.3g
Sodium	: 45mg

Pineapple & Spinach Juice

 Servings: 2

 Preparation Time: 10 minutes

Ingredients:

- 1 pineapple, peeled and chopped roughly
- 4 cups fresh baby spinach leaves
- 1 tablespoon fresh lemon juice

Instructions:

1. Add all the ingredients in a juicer and extract the juice according to the manufacturer's method.
2. Pour into two glasses and serve immediately.

Nutritional Information per Serving:

Calories	: 239
Fat	: 0.8g
Saturated Fat	: 0.1g
Carbohydrates	: 61.4g
Fiber	: 7.6g
Sugar	: 44.7g
Protein	: 4.2g
Sodium	: 54mg

Chapter 5: Plant-Based Juicing Recipes

Cucumber & Celery Juice

Servings: 2

Preparation Time: 10 minutes

Ingredients:

- 1 pound celery
- 2 large cucumbers, chopped roughly
- 2 teaspoons fresh lemon juice

Instructions:

1. Add all the ingredients in a juicer and extract the juice according to the manufacturer's method.
2. Pour into two glasses and serve immediately.

Nutritional Information per Serving:

Calories	: 83
Fat	: 0.8g
Saturated Fat	: 0.3g
Carbohydrates	: 17.8g
Fiber	: 5.2g
Sugar	: 8.2g
Protein	: 3.6g
Sodium	: 188mg

Heart Healthy Juices

What is meant by being hearth healthy? Any juice that can aid in controlling the blood cholesterol levels and keep our blood vessels healthy and elastic ensures good health for our heart. By consuming these juices, you will be having lots of phytonutrients, minerals, healthy fibers and vitamins which can best regulate the circulatory system.

Chapter 5: Plant-Based Juicing Recipes

Strawberry & Walnut Juice

Servings: 2

Preparation Time: 10 minutes

Ingredients:

- 4 cups fresh strawberries, hulled
- 3 tablespoons walnuts, chopped finely
- 4 fresh mint leaves
- 2 tablespoons maple syrup

Instructions:

1. Add all the ingredients in a juicer and extract the juice according to the manufacturer's method.
2. Pour into two glasses and serve immediately.

Nutritional Information per Serving:

Calories	: 193
Fat	: 5.5g
Saturated Fat	: 0.3g
Carbohydrates	: 36.4g
Fiber	: 6.4g
Sugar	: 26.1g
Protein	: 3.8g
Sodium	: 5mg

Berries & Apple Juice

Servings: 2

Preparation Time: 10 minutes

Ingredients:

- 1 cup fresh raspberries
- 1 cup fresh blueberries
- 1 cup fresh blackberries
- 3 large apples, cored and sliced

Instructions:

1. Add all the ingredients in a juicer and extract the juice according to the manufacturer's method.
2. Pour into two glasses and serve immediately.

Nutritional Information per Serving:

Calories	: 278
Fat	: 1.6g
Saturated Fat	: 0g
Carbohydrates	: 71g
Fiber	: 17.7g
Sugar	: 48.2g
Protein	: 3.2g
Sodium	: 5mg

Chapter 5: Plant-Based Juicing Recipes

Green Fruit Juice

Servings: 2

Preparation Time: 10 minutes

Ingredients:

- 4 large kiwis, peeled and chopped roughly
- 2 large green apples, cored and sliced
- 1 cup seedless green grapes
- 2 teaspoons lime juice

Instructions:

1. Add all the ingredients n a juicer and extract the juice according to the manufacturer's method.
2. Transfer into two glasses and serve immediately.

Nutritional Information per Serving:

Calories	: 240
Fat	: 1.4g
Saturated Fat	: 0.1g
Carbohydrates	: 61g
Fiber	: 10.4g
Sugar	: 44.3g
Protein	: 2.6g
Sodium	: 7mg

Apple, Celery & Ginger Juice

Servings: 2

Preparation Time: 10 minutes

Ingredients:

- 4 large green apples, cored and sliced
- 5 celery stalks
- 1 (1-inch) piece fresh ginger, peeled

Instructions:

1. Add all the ingredients in a juicer and extract the juice according to the manufacturer's method.
2. Pour into two glasses and serve immediately.

Nutritional Information per Serving:

Calories	: 242
Fat	: 0.9g
Saturated Fat	: 0g
Carbohydrates	: 63.5g
Fiber	: 11.6g
Sugar	: 47g
Protein	: 1.6g
Sodium	: 38mg

Chapter 5: Plant-Based Juicing Recipes

Kale & Orange Juice

Servings: 2

Preparation Time: 10 minutes

Ingredients:

- 4 cups fresh kale
- 5 oranges, peeled and sectioned

Instructions:

1. Add all the ingredients in a juicer and extract the juice according to the manufacturer's method.
2. Pour into two glasses and serve immediately.

Nutritional Information per Serving:

Calories	: 282
Fat	: 0.6g
Saturated Fat	: 0.1g
Carbohydrates	: 68.1g
Fiber	: 13g
Sugar	: 43g
Protein	: 8.3g
Sodium	: 58mg

Immunity Boost Juices

Our immune system is composed of an interlinking network of enzyme-producing glands and lymphatic system. They all work together to fight the harmful intruders. So, these juices are enriched with elements that can strengthen the immune system to produce more healthy cells to fight bacteria and viruses. A healthy immune system means lesser seasonal diseases and quick chances of recovery.

Chapter 5: Plant-Based Juicing Recipes

Blueberry, Beet & Apple Juice

Servings: 2

Preparation Time: 10 minutes

Ingredients:

- 1 cup fresh blueberries
- 3 large apples, cored and sliced
- 2 celery stalks
- 2 beets, trimmed and peeled
- 1 tablespoon fresh lime juice

Instructions:

1. Add all the ingredients in a juicer and extract the juice according to the manufacturer's method.
2. Pour into two glasses and serve immediately.

Nutritional Information per Serving:

Calories	: 263
Fat	: 1.1g
Saturated Fat	: 0g
Carbohydrates	: 67.2g
Fiber	: 12.1g
Sugar	: 50.2g
Protein	: 3.3g
Sodium	: 94mg

Apple, Beet & Carrot Juice

Servings: 2

Preparation Time: 10 minutes

Ingredients:

- 3 large carrots, peeled and chopped roughly
- 3 medium red beets, trimmed, peeled and chopped roughly
- 1 large Granny Smith apple, cored and sliced
- 1 large green apple, cored and sliced

Instructions:

1. Add all the ingredients in a juicer and extract the juice according to the manufacturer's method.
2. Pour into two glasses and serve immediately.

Nutritional Information per Serving:

Calories	: 226
Fat	: 0.7g
Saturated Fat	: 0g
Carbohydrates	: 56.4g
Fiber	: 11.1g
Sugar	: 40.5g
Protein	: 4g
Sodium	: 192mg

The Plant-Based Vegan: Juicing and Smoothie Diet Cookbook
200 Delicious Smoothie & Juicing Recipes To Lose Weight, Detox Your Body, and Live A Long Healthy Life

Chapter 5: Plant-Based Juicing Recipes

Citrus Spinach & Celery Juice

Servings: 2

Preparation Time: 10 minutes

Ingredients:

- 3 cups fresh spinach, chopped roughly
- 2 large celery stalks, chopped roughly
- 2 large green apples, cored and sliced
- 1 large orange, peeled, seeded and sectioned
- 1 tablespoon fresh lime juice
- 1 tablespoon fresh lemon juice

Instructions:

1. Add all the ingredients in a juicer and extract the juice according to the manufacturer's method.
2. Pour into two glasses and serve immediately.

Nutritional Information per Serving:

Calories	: 175
Fat	: 0.8g
Saturated Fat	: 0.1g
Carbohydrates	: 44g
Fiber	: 8.9g
Sugar	: 32.4g
Protein	: 2.9g
Sodium	: 53mg

Beet & Carrot Juice

Servings: 2

Preparation Time: 10 minutes

Ingredients:

- 5-6 large carrots, peeled and chopped roughly
- 5 large beets, trimmed, peeled and chopped roughly
- 1 (½-inch) piece fresh ginger, peeled

Instructions:

1. Add all the ingredients in a juicer and extract the juice according to the manufacturer's method.
2. Pour into two glasses and serve immediately.

Nutritional Information per Serving:

Calories	: 184
Fat	: 0.5g
Saturated Fat	: 0.1g
Carbohydrates	: 42.7g
Fiber	: 9.4g
Sugar	: 28.8g
Protein	: 5.7g
Sodium	: 316mg

Chapter 5: Plant-Based Juicing Recipes

Kale, Carrot & Apple Juice

Servings: 2

Preparation Time: 10 minutes

Ingredients:

- 3 cups fresh kale
- 3 large green apples, cored and sliced
- 3 large carrots, peeled and sectioned
- 1 large celery stalk
- 1 teaspoon fresh lemon juice

Instructions:

1. Add all the ingredients in a juicer and extract the juice according to the manufacturer's method.
2. Pour into two glasses and serve immediately.

Nutritional Information per Serving:

Calories	: 270
Fat	: 0.6g
Saturated Fat	: 0g
Carbohydrates	: 67.6g
Fiber	: 12.4g
Sugar	: 40.3g
Protein	: 4.9g
Sodium	: 128mg

Internal/ Structure Supporting Juices

These juices are prepared to aid the process of rejuvenation in the body. Our body cells constantly phase the process of ageing and then death. The formation of new and healthy cells, quickly and timely, can ensure good health. The more the new cells are formed, the healthier and more active you will become.

Chapter 5: Plant-Based Juicing Recipes

Swiss Chard, Apple & Orange Juice

Servings: 2

Preparation Time: 10 minutes

Ingredients:

- 3 cups Swiss chard
- 3 apples, cored and sliced
- 2 oranges, peeled and sectioned

Instructions:

1. Add all the ingredients in a juicer and extract the juice according to the manufacturer's method.
2. Pour into two glasses and serve immediately.

Nutritional Information per Serving:

Calories	: 271
Fat	: 1g
Saturated Fat	: 0g
Carbohydrates	: 69.8g
Fiber	: 13.4g
Sugar	: 52.6g
Protein	: 3.6g
Sodium	: 119mg

Red Fruit Juice

Servings: 2

Preparation Time: 10 minutes

Ingredients:

- 3 cups watermelon cut into large cubes
- 1 cup strawberries, hulled
- 3 large apples, cored and sliced
- 2 teaspoons fresh lemon juice

Instructions:

1. Add all the ingredients in a juicer and extract the juice according to the manufacturer's method.
2. Pour into two glasses and serve immediately.

Nutritional Information per Serving:

Calories	: 267
Fat	: 1.2g
Saturated Fat	: 0.2g
Carbohydrates	: 69g
Fiber	: 10.5g
Sugar	: 52.4g
Protein	: 2.8g
Sodium	: 8mg

The Plant-Based Vegan: Juicing and Smoothie Diet Cookbook
200 Delicious Smoothie & Juicing Recipes To Lose Weight, Detox Your Body, and Live A Long Healthy Life

Kale, Celery & Pear Juice

Servings: 2

Preparation Time: 10 minutes

Ingredients:

- 6 pears, cored and chopped roughly
- 3 celery stalks
- 3 cups fresh kale
- 2 tablespoons fresh parsley

Instructions:

1. Add all the ingredients in a juicer and extract the juice according to the manufacturer's method.
2. Pour into two glasses and serve immediately.

Nutritional Information per Serving:

Calories	: 209
Fat	: 0.9g
Saturated Fat	: 0.1g
Carbohydrates	: 50.5g
Fiber	: 15.2g
Sugar	: 26.2g
Protein	: 5.1g
Sodium	: 66mg

Mixed Veggies Juice

Servings: 2

Preparation Time: 10 minutes

Ingredients:

- 2 cups fresh kale
- 1 cup fresh tomatoes
- 1 carrot, peeled and chopped roughly
- 1 cucumber, chopped roughly
- 1 celery stalk, chopped roughly
- 2 tablespoons fresh lime juice

Instructions:

1. Add all the ingredients in a juicer and extract the juice according to the manufacturer's method.
2. Pour into two glasses and serve immediately.

Nutritional Information per Serving:

Calories	: 87
Fat	: 0.4g
Saturated Fat	: 0.1g
Carbohydrates	: 19.4g
Fiber	: 3.7g
Sugar	: 6.5g
Protein	: 4.1g
Sodium	: 64mg

Spinach, Celery, Apple & Orange Juice

Servings: 2

Preparation Time: 10 minutes

Ingredients:

- 3 cups fresh spinach, chopped roughly
- 2 large celery stalks, chopped roughly
- 2 large green apples, cored and sliced
- 1 large orange, peeled and sectioned
- 1 tablespoon fresh lime juice
- 1 tablespoon fresh lemon juice

Instructions:

1. Add all the ingredients in a juicer and extract the juice according to the manufacturer's method.
2. Pour into two glasses and serve immediately.

Nutritional Information per Serving:

Calories	: 214
Fat	: 0.6g
Saturated Fat	: 0.1g
Carbohydrates	: 52.9g
Fiber	: 9.4g
Sugar	: 32.2g
Protein	: 4.6g
Sodium	: 61mg

Green Juices

Made out of the blend of a variety of green vegetables and some fruits juices, these juices are the reservoirs of essential minerals and antioxidants. Anyone aiming to improve their digestive system, boost immunity and cleanse blood should consume these green juices. These juices are low in calories and carbs, and for this reason, they are considered effective for weight loss or weight management.

Chapter 5: Plant-Based Juicing Recipes

Apple, Cucumber & Kale Juice

🍽 **Servings:** 2

🕐 **Preparation Time:** 10 minutes

Ingredients:

- 2½ cups fresh kale leaves
- ½ cup fresh parsley leaves and stems
- 1 medium green apple, cored and chopped roughly
- 1 large seedless English cucumber, rinsed
- 1 (1-inch) piece fresh ginger, peeled
- 1 medium lemon, halved

Instructions:

1. Add all the ingredients in a juicer and extract the juice according to the manufacturer's method.
2. Pour into two glasses and serve immediately.

Nutritional Information per Serving:

Calories	: 100
Fat	: 0.7g
Saturated Fat	: 0.1g
Carbohydrates	: 24.5g
Fiber	: 5.1g
Sugar	: 14.6g
Protein	: 3g
Sodium	: 42mg

Kale, Pear & Grapefruit Juice

🍽 **Servings:** 2

🕐 **Preparation Time:** 10 minutes

Ingredients:

- 2 large pears, cored and sliced
- 2 grapefruit, peeled and sectioned
- 2 cups fresh kale
- 1 (1-inch) piece fresh ginger, peeled

Instructions:

1. Add all the ingredients in a juicer and extract the juice according to the manufacturer's method.
2. Pour into two glasses and serve immediately.

Nutritional Information per Serving:

Calories	: 198
Fat	: 0.5g
Saturated Fat	: 0g
Carbohydrates	: 49.8g
Fiber	: 9g
Sugar	: 29.3g
Protein	: 3.6g
Sodium	: 32mg

Chapter 5: Plant-Based Juicing Recipes

Green Veggies & Fruit Juice

Servings: 2

Preparation Time: 10 minutes

Ingredients:

- 2 small green apples, cored and sliced
- 2 small pears, cored and sliced
- 3 cups fresh spinach leaves
- 6 medium celery stalks, chopped roughly
- 1 lemon, peeled and seeded

Instructions:

1. Add all the ingredients in a juicer and extract the juice according to the manufacturer's method.
2. Pour into two glasses and serve immediately.

Nutritional Information per Serving:

Calories	: 258
Fat	: 1g
Saturated Fat	: 0.1g
Carbohydrates	: 66.5g
Fiber	: 13.9g
Sugar	: 44.6g
Protein	: 3.1g
Sodium	: 81mg

Kale, Spinach, Pear & Fennel Juice

 Servings: 2

 **Preparation Time:** 10 minutes

Ingredients:

- 3 pears, cored and sliced
- 2 cups fresh kale
- 2 cups fresh spinach
- 1 fennel bulb, chopped
- 1 (½-inch) piece fresh ginger, peeled

Instructions:

1. Add all the ingredients in a juicer and extract the juice according to the manufacturer's method.
2. Pour into two glasses and serve immediately.

Nutritional Information per Serving:

Calories	: 270
Fat	: 0.7g
Saturated Fat	: 0g
Carbohydrates	: 67.4g
Fiber	: 15g
Sugar	: 30.6g
Protein	: 5.7g
Sodium	: 108mg

The Plant-Based Vegan: Juicing and Smoothie Diet Cookbook
200 Delicious Smoothie & Juicing Recipes To Lose Weight, Detox Your Body, and Live A Long Healthy Life

Chapter 5: Plant-Based Juicing Recipes

Apple, Celery & Herbs Juice

- Servings: 2
- Preparation Time: 10 minutes

Ingredients:

- 2 large Granny Smith apples, cored and sliced
- 8 celery stalks
- ¼ cup fresh parsley
- ¼ cup fresh cilantro
- (1-inch) piece fresh ginger
- 2 teaspoons fresh lemon juice

Instructions:

1. Add all the ingredients in a juicer and extract the juice according to the manufacturer's method.
2. Pour into two glasses and serve immediately.

Nutritional Information per Serving:

Calories	: 76
Fat	: 0.5g
Saturated Fat	: 0.1g
Carbohydrates	: 18.7g
Fiber	: 4.2g
Sugar	: 12.7
Protein	: 1.2g
Sodium	: 62mg

Apple, Celery & Cucumber Juice

- Servings: 2
- Preparation Time: 10 minutes

Ingredients:

- 2 large green apples, cored and sliced
- 4 celery stalks
- 2 large cucumbers
- 1 (1-inch) piece fresh ginger, peeled

Instructions:

1. Add all the ingredients in a juicer and extract the juice according to the manufacturer's method.
2. Pour into two glasses and serve immediately.

Nutritional Information per Serving:

Calories	: 167
Fat	: 0.8g
Saturated Fat	: 0.1g
Carbohydrates	: 42.7g
Fiber	: 7.5g
Sugar	: 28.7g
Protein	: 2.8g
Sodium	: 35mg

Chapter 5: Plant-Based Juicing Recipes

Pear & Kiwi Juice

Servings: 2

Preparation Time: 10 minutes

Ingredients:

- 4 pears, cored and sliced
- 4 kiwi fruit, peeled and sliced
- 2 celery stalks
- 2 tablespoons fresh lemon juice

Instructions:

1. Add all the ingredients in a juicer and extract the juice according to the manufacturer's method.
2. Pour into two glasses and serve immediately.

Nutritional Information per Serving:

Calories	: 270
Fat	: 0.7g
Saturated Fat	: 0g
Carbohydrates	: 67.4g
Fiber	: 15g
Sugar	: 30.6g
Protein	: 5.7g
Sodium	: 108mg

Kale, Cucumber & Parsley Juice

Servings: 2

Preparation Time: 10 minutes

Ingredients:

- 4 cups fresh baby kale
- 2 large seedless cucumbers, chopped roughly
- ½ cup fresh parsley
- 1 (1-inch) piece fresh ginger, peeled
- 1 lemon, halved

Instructions:

1. Add all the ingredients in a juicer and extract the juice according to the manufacturer's method.
2. Pour into two glasses and serve immediately.

Nutritional Information per Serving:

Calories	: 120
Fat	: 0.5g
Saturated Fat	: 0.2g
Carbohydrates	: 26.5g
Fiber	: 4.1g
Sugar	: 5.2g
Protein	: 6.5g
Sodium	: 73mg

Chapter 5: Plant-Based Juicing Recipes

Greens, Celery & Carrot Juice

Servings: 2

Preparation Time: 10 minutes

Ingredients:

- 3 cups fresh kale
- 2 cup fresh arugula
- 1 large carrot, peeled and chopped roughly
- 2 celery stalks
- 1 lemon, halved
- 1 (1-inch) piece fresh ginger, peeled

Instructions:

1. Add all the ingredients in a juicer and extract the juice according to the manufacturer's method.
2. Pour into two glasses and serve immediately.

Nutritional Information per Serving:

Calories	: 77
Fat	: 0.2g
Saturated Fat	: 0.1g
Carbohydrates	: 16.7g
Fiber	: 3.3g
Sugar	: 2.6g
Protein	: 4.1g
Sodium	: 88mg

Kale & Celery Juice

Servings: 2

Preparation Time: 10 minutes

Ingredients:

- 4 celery stalks
- 5 cups fresh kale leaves
- 1 (½-inch) piece fresh ginger, peeled
- 1 lime, halved

Instructions:

1. Add all the ingredients in a juicer and extract the juice according to the manufacturer's method.
2. Pour into two glasses and serve immediately.

Nutritional Information per Serving:

Calories	: 91
Fat	: 0.1g
Saturated Fat	: 0g
Carbohydrates	: 19.8g
Fiber	: 3.4g
Sugar	: 0.6g
Protein	: 5.3g
Sodium	: 100mg

Conclusion

So, how did you like the plant-based smoothies and juices recipes shared in this cookbook? Do they seem delicious and healthy? Well, give them a try and introduce them to your weekly menu. You can mix and match different recipes for the day to enjoy more flavors and variety. For instance, you can have a vegan smoothie in the morning and a juice between lunch and dinner time, or you can have a smoothie during snack time. There are several incentives to choose a plant-based diet, the first being the health benefits it guarantees. To convince yourself, first imagine all the nutrients which can be sourced from a plant-based diet that includes unsaturated fats, high amount fibers, and minerals along with a balanced proportion of macronutrients.

Plant-based food is full of phytonutrients; these are special chemicals present only in plants and serve as the antioxidants and detoxifiers in the human body. When the entire diet consists of plant-based items, there is an increased intake of these phytonutrients, which helps the body resist cancer and other health-affecting agents. Since a plant-based diet is free from all saturated fats, it is excellent for people suffering from high blood cholesterol. The plant-based oils do not increase cholesterol but provide high-density lipoproteins- the good fats. It also controls obesity and helps to achieve weight loss. Similarly, the diet has also proven to control the body mass index in perfect balance through its nutritional contents.

This cookbook provided you with all the essential smoothies and juices ideas to incorporate a plant-based diet into your routine with complete ease and comfort. So, mark your favorite recipes now, and lets get started!

Index of Ingredients

A

agave nectar, 79, 85
almond butter, 54, 88, 94, 106, 120, 121, 132,
almond milk, 36, 54, 55, 56, 57, 60, 63, 67, 68, 69, 72, 73, 74, 75, 76, 78, 79, 80, 81, 82, 84, 85, 86, 88, 90, 91, 92, 93, 94, 96, 97, 98, 99, 100, 102, 103, 104, 106, 108, 110, 111, 114, 117, 120, 121, 122,123, 124, 126, 132, 133, 134, 136, 137, 139, 140, 141
almonds, 54, 59, 63, 102
aloe vera, 144
apple, 31, 40, 48, 55, 64, 66, 67, 75, 87, 110, 117, 118, 124, 133, 142, 143, 146, 147, 150, 153, 154, 155, 156, 162, 163, 166, 168, 170, 172, 174, 176
apricots, 129
arugula, 27, 39, 178
avocado, 58, 61, 63, 76, 77, 82, 88, 90, 91, 93, 100, 106, 108, 110, 112, 118, 142

B

baby greens, 92, 94
baby kale, 63, 74, 94, 106, 142, 177
baby spinach, 58, 64, 88, 94, 106, 111, 143, 159
banana, 54, 55, 57, 60, 61, 62, 67, 69, 70, 72, 73, 74, 75, 76, 79, 81, 85, 86, 87, 88, 96, 97, 98, 102, 103,105, 106, 109, 110, 111, 114, 116, 117, 118, 120, 121, 122, 123, 124, 126, 128, 129, 134, 140, 141
basil leaves, 87, 117
beet, 78, 79, 96, 148, 166, 167
berries, 18, 31, 32, 33, 34, 40, 56, 61, 65, 71, 78, 80, 87, 104, 147, 162
blackberries, 31, 34, 56, 62, 72, 74, 75, 162
blue spirulina powder, 78
blueberries, 31, 34, 38, 53, 61, 64, 66, 69, 78, 79, 80, 96, 136, 146, 147, 162, 166
broccoli, 18, 24, 27, 38, 64, 94, 155
broccoli florets, 64, 94

C

cacao powder, 23, 32, 60, 72, 122, 123, 124, 137
cane sugar, 146
carrot, 28, 99, 100, 106, 114, 115, 139, 147, 148, 149, 152, 153, 154, 156, 159, 166, 167, 168, 171, 178
cashews, 114, 116
cauliflower florets, 100
celery, 27, 38, 77, 81, 82, 115, 118, 139, 149, 150, 156, 160, 163, 166, 167, 168, 171, 172, 175, 176, 177, 178,
celery stalk, 81, 82, 139, 168, 171
cherries, 31, 69, 73, 80, 124, 139
chia seeds, 32, 54, 60, 61, 66, 72, 73, 75, 79, 82, 84, 91, 94, 98, 102, 103, 116, 122, 123, 124, 133, 137
cilantro, 29, 39, 87, 150, 176
coconut butter, 60, 105
coconut cream, 104
coconut oil, 78, 106, 117
coconut sugar, 158
coconut water, 30, 36, 66, 73, 97, 98, 99, 109, 112, 116, 118, 124, 129, 130, 142
coconut yogurt, 55, 57, 73, 75, 79, 91, 103, 124, 133, 135
coffee, 23, 34, 60, 122, 137
cold green tea, 84
cranberries, 38, 53, 67, 85, 130, 147
cranberry juice, 61
cucumber, 28, 39, 66, 70, 82, 85, 88, 92, 93, 112, 127, 128, 129, 143, 150, 156, 160, 171, 174, 176, 177

D

dates, 23, 61, 72, 73, 74, 85, 99, 102, 116, 121, 122, 137

F

fennel bulb, 175
flax oil, 106
flaxseed meal, 76, 112
flaxseed, 67, 76, 96, 100, 112, 117, 118
frozen mixed berries, 56
frozen strawberries, 55, 67, 75, 81, 86, 90, 117, 126, 137, 140, 143
full-fat coconut milk, 58, 62

G

ginger, 39, 62, 81, 82, 84, 93, 97, 98, 100, 102, 104, 105, 112, 114, 115, 116, 127, 130, 135, 141, 148, 149, 150, 152, 154, 156, 163, 167, 174, 175, 176, 177, 178
goji berries, 33, 80
goji berry powder, 74
grapefruit, 51, 85, 86, 149, 153, 174
green bell pepper, 94
green cabbage, 70, 94
green grape juice, 104
green spirulina powder, 61, 82
green tea, 18, 34, 36, 84, 91, 106, 126, 149, 151
ground black pepper, 84, 139, 154, 158
ground cardamom, 84, 97, 116
ground cinnamon, 55, 58, 60, 66, 72, 84, 92, 94, 98, 102, 105, 106, 133, 135, 139
ground cloves, 94
ground flaxseeds, 33, 74, 103
guava, 128

H

hemp hearts, 111
hemp protein powder, 81
hemp seeds, 32, 33, 58, 62, 63, 75, 79, 86, 108, 123, 124, 126, 134

K

kale, 18, 27, 38, 61, 63, 64, 70, 74, 77, 82, 87, 88, 94, 106, 110, 111, 118, 126, 142, 149, 150, 164, 168, 171, 174, 175, 177, 178
kale leaves, 61, 64, 88, 110, 174, 178
kiwi, 18, 31, 57, 104, 111, 114, 117, 127, 135, 177
kiwis, 57, 163

L

lemon, 18, 30, 46, 47, 51, 85, 88, 93, 99, 109, 110, 117, 118, 128, 139, 146, 148, 149, 150, 151, 153, 154, 156, 159, 160, 167, 168, 170, 172, 174, 175, 176, 177, 178
lemon juice, 46, 85, 88, 93, 99, 109, 110, 117, 118, 128, 139, 149, 153, 154, 159, 160, 167, 168, 170, 172, 176, 177
lettuce leaves, 76, 112
lime, 18, 47, 51, 62, 66, 86, 87, 90, 91, 92, 96, 104, 108, 111, 112, 129, 142, 146, 150, 151, 163, 166, 167, 171, 172, 178
lime juice, 62, 66, 86, 87, 90, 91, 92, 96, 104, 108, 111, 112, 129, 142, 146, 163, 166, 167, 171, 172
lime zest, 62, 108
liquid stevia, 54, 58, 63, 64, 66, 67, 78, 80, 104, 105, 110, 112, 132, 139, 142
lucuma powder, 60

M

maca powder, 73, 78, 102, 123, 135
mango, 18, 31, 57, 62, 111, 115, 116, 118, 121, 134, 140, 141
maple syrup, 37, 54, 58, 60, 62, 66, 68, 69, 74, 76, 80, 87, 97, 98, 103, 108, 109, 111, 116, 124, 127, 128, 129, 133, 135, 136, 140, 162
matcha green tea powder, 91, 106
matcha tea powder, 64
MCT oil, 84, 93, 104
Medjool dates, 61, 73, 74, 85, 102, 121
melon, 31, 104, 128, 141
mint leaves, 56, 76, 88, 90, 92, 96, 98, 108, 112, 128, 129, 155, 162
mixed berries, 56, 87
mixed greens, 71, 81
mustard greens, 87

N

natural immune support, 84
nutritional yeast, 132, 134

O

oats, 42, 46, 53, 54, 55, 60, 78, 97, 122, 133, 135
old-fashioned oats, 54, 55
orange, 32, 33, 36, 47, 56, 57, 58, 70, 75, 85, 96, 100, 105, 106, 114, 115, 117, 126, 130, 140, 143, 147, 152, 155, 156, 159, 164, 167, 170, 172
orange juice, 56, 57, 70, 75, 85, 96, 105, 106, 114, 115, 117, 140, 143, 147, 152, 156, 164, 170, 172

P

papaya, 41, 76, 98, 99
parsley, 27, 29, 38, 39, 87, 93, 97, 118, 127, 149, 155, 171, 174, 176, 177
peach, 31, 68, 69, 98, 114, 140
peaches, 38, 53, 68, 69, 98, 140
peanut butter, 54, 103, 122, 132, 134, 137
pear, 73, 97, 98, 109, 118, 130, 142, 171, 174, 175, 177
pecans, 102
pineapple, 31, 36, 41, 48, 57, 68, 70, 79, 84, 85, 86, 96, 97, 106, 118, 128, 159
pistachios, 73, 120
plum, 126
pomegranate juice, 79, 80, 87, 154, 158
pomegranate seeds, 80, 154, 158
psyllium seeds, 63
pumpkin, 28, 56, 64, 105, 111, 136
pumpkin pie spice, 105, 136
pumpkin puree, 105
pumpkin seeds, 56, 64, 111

R

raspberries, 31, 68, 74, 78, 79, 81, 103, 116, 127, 129, 133, 147, 162
raw hemp seeds, 58, 63
raw pistachios, 73
raw wheat germ, 64, 106
red bell pepper, 67, 155
red cabbage, 80, 127
rolled oats, 60, 78, 97, 122, 133
romaine lettuce, 112, 118

S

salt, 46, 60, 96, 130, 137, 139, 158
seedless green grapes, 109, 111, 142, 163
silken tofu, 68, 136
soy milk, 62
soy protein powder, 103
spinach, 18, 27, 38, 56, 58, 63, 64, 77, 87, 88, 90, 91, 92, 93, 94, 100, 106, 109, 111, 118, 124, 126, 130, 137, 143, 148, 159, 167, 172, 175, 180
spinach leaves, 27, 56, 159, 175
stevia powder, 84, 133, 136
strawberries, 31, 53, 55, 67, 73, 75, 78, 81, 86, 90, 117, 121, 123, 126, 134, 137, 140, 143, 146, 147, 155, 162, 170
sunflower butter, 93, 135
sunflower seed butter, 93
sunflower seeds, 56, 73, 135
sweet potato, 105, 115, 147
sweet potato puree, 105
Swiss chard, 27, 38, 87, 109, 150, 170

T

tomato, 28, 117, 127, 139, 155
tomatoes, 28, 38, 117, 139, 171
turmeric, 29, 62, 84, 102, 105, 116

U

unflavored collagen protein powder, 93
unflavored vegan protein powder, 69
unsweetened cherries, 69
unsweetened coconut milk, 56, 70, 76, 91, 105, 123
unsweetened ground coconut, 130
unsweetened hemp milk, 121, 134
unsweetened protein powder, 67, 104
unsweetened soy milk, 61, 122, 135, 136
unsweetened vegan protein powder, 66, 68, 70, 72, 105, 106, 120, 122, 132, 133, 134, 135, 136
unsweetened vegan vanilla protein powder, 111, 121, 132, 134

V

vanilla extract, 54, 56, 57, 62, 67, 72, 90, 93, 103, 104, 114, 116, 120, 123, 132, 135, 136
vegan dark chocolate chips, 81
vegan protein powder, 35, 53, 124, 131

W

walnuts, 34, 59, 60, 63, 72, 102, 121, 162
watermelon, 75, 86, 129, 158, 170

Z

zucchini, 28, 92

References

10 reasons Why JUICING can improve your life. The Body Toolkit. (n.d.). https://www.thebodytoolkit.com/blog-article/10-reasons-why-juicing-can-improve-your-life.

23 important benefits of Drinking Healthy Smoothies. Neighborhood Jam. (2019, May 2). https://thatsmyjamok.com/23-important-benefits-of-drinking-healthy-smoothies/.

6 Pack Fitness. (2015, March 5). *Try these 8 Best greens for smoothies*. 6 Pack Fitness. https://www.sixpackbags.com/blogs/news/best-greens-for-smoothies.

Admin. (2019, December 8). *Best vegetables to add to smoothies*. me time away. https://www.metimeaway.com/magazine/best-vegetables-to-add-to-smoothies/.

Amidor, Toby. "Healthy How-to: Juicing Fruits & Veggies." *Food Network*, 2010, www.foodnetwork.com/healthyeats/healthy-tips/2009/05/healthy-how-to-juicing-fruits-and-veggies.

Best superfoods to add to smoothies. Running on Real Food. (2020, April 17). https://runningonrealfood.com/best-superfoods-to-add-to-smoothies/.

Best veggies to add to smoothies + choco-zucchini smoothie. Running on Real Food. (2020, November 25). https://runningonrealfood.com/best-vegetables-to-add-to-smoothies/.

BS;, Uckoo RM;Jayaprakasha GK;Balasubramaniam VM;Patil. "Grapefruit (Citrus Paradisi Macfad) PHYTOCHEMICALS Composition Is Modulated by Household Processing Techniques." *Journal of Food Science*, U.S. National Library of Medicine, 2012, pubmed.ncbi.nlm.nih.gov/22957912/.

Clark, S. (2017, June 15). *Smoothies vs Juicing- which one is better for your health?* HuffPost. https://www.huffpost.com/entry/smoothies-vs-juicing-which-one-is-better-for-your_b_59424cfbe4b04c03fa261830.

Curley, K. (2020, January 21). *List of fruits and vegetables that can be used in smoothies*. Healthy Eating | SF Gate. https://healthyeating.sfgate.com/list-fruits-vegetables-can-used-smoothies-2785.html.

Fernandez, M., & Maria FernandezA nutritionist student who loves to mix match ingredients to get the perfect balanced food. She believes that everyone should understand the basic contains of food and how to process it correctly. (2020, December 3). *The best liquid bases to put in your smoothies*. NavanFoods. https://www.navanfoods.com/best-liquids-for-smoothies/.

Healthline. (2019, July 6). *The 12 best vegetables to juice*. EcoWatch. https://www.ecowatch.com/best-vegetables-to-juice-2639094307.html.

Jen Hansard and Jadah Sellner for RodaleWellness.com. (2019, June 12). *8 herbs and spices you should add to Your smoothies*. Prevention. https://www.prevention.com/food-nutrition/a20485305/add-these-8-herbs-spices-to-your-smoothies/.

Killeen, B. L. (n.d.). *Healthy smoothies: BEST Smoothie ingredients & 10 to ditch*. EatingWell. https://www.eatingwell.com/article/277310/healthy-smoothies-best-smoothie-ingredients-10-to-ditch/.

Leftover juice pulp gets a second life with these diys. Vegetarian Times. (2021, May 20). https://www.vegetariantimes.com/vegan-vegetarian-recipes/vegan-recipes/what-do-i-do-with-leftover-juice-pulp/.

Mather, Katrina. "10 Reasons Why JUICING Can Improve Your Life." *The Body Toolkit*, Oct. 2014, www.thebodytoolkit.com/blog-article/10-reasons-why-juicing-can-improve-your-life.

Robinf. (2020, December 30). *11 creative ways to use LEFTOVER Juice pulp*. Goodnature. https://www.goodnature.com/blog/11-creative-ways-to-use-leftover-juice-pulp/#creamcheese.

Schaefer, A. (2018, December 4). *Juicing vs. blending: Which is better for losing weight?* Healthline. https://www.healthline.com/health/food-nutrition/juicing-vs-blending#sugar.

Smoothie ingredients - list of fruit for smoothies. Enjoy Smoothies. (n.d.). https://www.enjoysmoothies.com/smoothie-ingredients-2.html.

Taylor, M. (2018, May 7). *10 superfoods that make the BEST Smoothie Ingredients*. Greatist. https://greatist.com/eat/superfoods-to-add-to-smoothies#1.

Usher, C. (2020, June 17). *What are health benefits of going dairy-free?* Fresh n' Lean. https://www.freshnlean.com/blog/real-reasons-part-2-going-dairy-free/#:~:text=Consuming%20less%20dairy%20may%20help%20your%20digestion&text=Many%20report%20stomach%20bloating%20and,make%20it%20easier%20to%20digest.